THE ORIGINS OF INFANT BAPTISM

STUDIES IN HISTORICAL THEOLOGY

THE ORIGINS
OF INFANT BAPTISM

A further study in reply to Kurt Aland

JOACHIM JEREMIAS

SCM PRESS LTD
BLOOMSBURY STREET LONDON

Translated by Dorothea M. Barton, M.A., from the German
Nochmals: Die Anfänge der Kindertaufe
(Chr. Kaiser Verlag, Munich, 1962)

FIRST PUBLISHED IN ENGLISH 1963
© SCM PRESS LTD 1963
PRINTED IN GREAT BRITAIN BY
W. & J. MACKAY & CO LTD, CHATHAM

CONTENTS

PREFACE

A DETAILED reply to my book *Infant Baptism in the First Four Centuries* (SCM Press, 1960, cited as J) has been made by Professor Kurt Aland in a treatise of his own: *Did the Early Church Baptize Infants?* (SCM Press, 1962, cited as A).

I would have preferred to meet this attack by silence. I hate controversy and unfortunately Aland, by the tone of his argument, did not make the decision to reply to him an easy one. But the subject obliges me to express my opinion. I must first emphasize the fact that I have learned quite a few things from Aland's book; I have learned still more by being forced to scrutinize all the sources thoroughly once again. I entered upon this task ready to admit any possible errors and to revise my conclusions, if necessary. Yet the need for such a revision did not arise. At each point I was confirmed in my conviction that there is no defence for the older conception, revived by Aland, that up to the end of the second century, and indeed even beyond it, children were not baptized until a mature age. Not only does this conception lack support from the sources, but, as I trust will become evident, it arose out of an understanding of baptism which came to be adopted during the second century and which is incompatible with that of the New Testament.

In the following exposition I have endeavoured to restrict the controversial element to the indispensable minimum and instead, as far as was possible, to carry the discussion further. For it is certainly not yet at an end. *Dies diem docet.* I will take this opportunity to mention that I have already revised in the English translation of my book (January 1960) the comments on I Cor. 7.14c; I no longer venture to deduce from this passage that in Corinth the children born in Christian marriage were not baptized.

I have to thank my friend Hermann Dörries, who was kind enough to read the manuscript before it was handed in, my assistant, Dr Berndt Schaller, and his successor, Dr Christoph Burchard, for help in procuring the literature as well as for helpful suggestions, and one of my students, Klaus-Peter Jörns, for preparing the book for the press.

As regards the English translation, I am indebted to the translator, Mrs Dorothea M. Barton, for her careful work, and to Dr Brian Gerrish of McCormick Theological Seminary, Chicago, for his comments on a number of difficult passages. Dr Burchard was again of great help.

ABBREVIATIONS

Arndt and Gingrich	W. F. Arndt and F. W. Gingrich, *A Greek–English Lexicon of the New Testament*, London and Chicago, 1957, being the ET of W. Bauer, *Griechisch-Deutsches Wörterbuch zu den Schriften des Neuen Testaments und der übrigen urchristlichen Literatur*[4], Berlin, 1952
BZNW	Beihefte zur *ZNW*, Giessen and Berlin
CC	Corpus Christianorum, Series Latina, Turnhout, Belgium
CSEL	Corpus Scriptorum Ecclesiasticorum Latinorum, Vienna
ET	English translation
GCS	Die Griechischen Christlichen Schriftsteller der ersten Jahrhunderte, Leipzig and Berlin
MPG	Migne, *Patrologia Graeca*, Paris
SB	*Sammelbuch Griechischer Urkunden aus Aegypten* . . . see p. 18 n. 1.
Str. Bill.	H. L. Strack and P. Billerbeck, *Kommentar zum Neuen Testament aus Talmud und Midrasch*, 5 vols. in 6, Munich, 1922–61
TU	Texte und Untersuchungen zur Geschichte der altchristlichen Literatur, Leipzig and Berlin
TWNT	*Theologisches Wörterbuch zum Neuen Testament*, ed. G. Kittel, Stuttgart, 1932ff.
ZNW	*Zeitschrift für die Neutestamentliche Wissenschaft*, Giessen and Berlin
'A	Aquila's translation of the Old Testament
Θ	Theodotion's translation of the Old Testament
Σ	Symmachus' translation of the Old Testament

I

Introduction

I. THE PROBLEM

ALAND SAYS in his preface that the result of his study of the problem of infant baptism in the early days of the primitive Church had been 'surprising, indeed dismaying' (A 9). Even though he did not claim that his interpretation of the sources in every detail was the only possible one, yet he was of the opinion 'that the result of his investigations, that infant baptism is certainly provable only from the third century, . . . cannot be contested from the sources' (A 10). As this dismaying conclusion represents the outcome of the long discussion of my work, every reader must inevitably gain the impression that I dispute this final 'result'. Why does Aland not at any point note the fact that exactly the same can be read in my book? It was with deliberate intention that I placed at the beginning of my book a seven-page survey of the sources and marked with an asterisk those texts which expressly mention the baptism of children. The first asterisk occurs on page 13 against Tertullian, *De baptismo* 18.3–6 (AD 200/6). By this means I wished to make it clear to the reader from the outset, before I myself wrote as much as a single word, that a distinction must be made between the direct and indirect evidence for the baptism of children and that direct statements do not appear in the sources until Tertullian. What Aland lays down as his final 'result' is the point from which I set out.[1]

No, there is no difference of opinion about the incontrovertible fact that direct evidence for the baptism of children starts only with

---

[1] When Aland goes even further and puts to me the question 'What *direct* [Aland's italics] statements remain to him from the early times concerning the baptism in infancy of children born to Christian parents?' (A 45, n. 1), I can read this only with astonishment. How can he expect me to name direct witnesses from the early period, after I have made it as clear as possible in the survey of the sources that these do not exist? If we possessed direct evidence from the first two centuries the whole debate would be settled!

Tertullian. We first begin to differ when we ask: what happened before this? Aland holds the opinion that during the first two centuries an age-limit was observed and that children were not baptized until a mature age; I myself consider that this hypothesis is not confirmed by the sources. What was the practice of the Church up to AD 200? *That* is the question on which everything turns.

* * *

At the same time we must not overlook the fact that Aland and I differ from each other about the definition of the problem. Whilst I examine the baptism of *children* (*Kindertaufe*) during the first four centuries, Aland restricts himself to the baptism of *infants* (*Säuglingstaufe*) in the New Testament and in the primitive Church. He justifies this limitation of the subject by saying: 'Only if we speak of the baptism of *infants* does the nature of the problem in the earliest days of the Church come clearly into focus, and only so can we gain an answer to the question we pose today' (A 46). To this I must say that it is in my opinion an extremely dubious proceeding to allow present-day problems to influence the way a subject is approached in historical research; for in that case there is a danger that an unbiased outlook on the historical facts is clouded and the discussion is simplified in a way which cannot be allowed (a typical example is found in A 73f.).

In order to prejudge nothing, I for my part deal with the baptism of *children* in the primitive Church and leave it to the sources to guide me to whatever conclusion they lead.[1] When Aland maintains: '[Jeremias] naturally means the baptism of infants. He is concerned to prove that this baptism of infants, even when they are the children of Christian parents, has continually been practised in the Church' (A 46), when he even speaks of my use of words to 'produce favourable associations' (A 73), I note such insinuations only with regret. I stated definitely in the preface to my book: 'It does not attempt to do more than lay before the reader the historical material . . . in as concrete and sober a manner as possible' (p. 9). Whether I have achieved my aim is not for me to judge. I am all the more grateful to M. Barth that in his review of my book he has

[1] Despite this broad basis of my investigation, the narrower term 'infant baptism' was used in the English titles of both my books, because it is as established in English as *Kindertaufe* is in German, and because it is quite in accordance with the results.

given me the credit for going, if anything, too far in the attempt not to suppress such evidence as might run counter to my thesis.[1]

2. THE METHOD EMPLOYED

Until 1928 it was generally held that infant baptism came into vogue only in the second half of the second century. This conclusion seemed to be incontrovertible, since we do not possess direct evidence for the earlier period. But in 1928 doubts began to appear, actually prompted by the comparative study of religions. It was A. Oepke who, taking up suggestions of J. Leipoldt,[2] asserted that both in the Hellenistic environment (initiation of children in the mysteries) as well as in Judaism (baptism of the children of proselytes when whole families were converted) circumstances were at work which might induce the primitive Church, too, to baptize children.[3] This set in motion a new way of considering the matter which no longer traced the argument back from the direct witnesses, but moved forward from the New Testament and its environment. I myself have followed in my book this new method of handling the question. By contrast K. Aland is again pursuing the other course which starts the inquiry at about AD 200 and works backward. There would be no objection to this method if it did not result in Aland's assuming—without noticing it—that the age of the New Testament also accepted that stunted conception of baptism held by popular Hellenistic Christianity in the second century. If only to avoid such errors I adhere to the method which works forward.

[1] *Theologische Literaturzeitung* 85, 1960, col. 42.
[2] My colleague Albrecht Oepke, who died on 10 December, 1955, expressly asked me in a letter of 20 September, 1949, to make this acknowledgement.
[3] 'Zur Frage nach dem Ursprung der Kindertaufe' in *Das Erbe Martin Luthers und die gegenwärtige theologische Forschung* (L. Ihmels-Festschrift), Leipzig, 1928, 84–100.

II

The Baptism of 'Houses'

1. THE NEW TESTAMENT PASSAGES

IT IS well known that the New Testament repeatedly mentions that 'households' are devout (Acts 10.2), receive salvation (11.14; 16.31), become believers (John 4.53; Acts 18.8) and are baptized (I Cor. 1.16; Acts 16.15, cf. 33 οἱ αὐτοῦ ἅπαντες). Several times additions such as 'the whole' (πᾶς, ὅλος) and alternative phrases such as 'all his people' (οἱ αὐτοῦ ἅπαντες), 'with the entire house' (πανοικεί), are used to express the fact that no single member of the household was left out. The house in the narrower sense includes, as we shall see: the father of the family, the mother of the family and the children of every age; in the wider sense the relations living in the house were also reckoned in, but not the servants without further comment. It is natural to conclude from this that the references to the 'whole' household are intended in the first place to include the children. We do not assert that in each case children were, in fact, actually present. But we do mean that Paul and Luke could under no circumstances have used the phrase, 'a household' or 'his whole family' were baptized, if they had wished to say that only adults had been baptized (J 21-22).

In section 8, 'The "*Oikos*-formula"' (A 87-94), Aland has vigorously contradicted these statements in my book. This section seems to me to be certainly the weakest in Aland's work. It must be said frankly that here he has made the argument too simple for himself.

There are two possible ways of trying to evade the conclusion just outlined. The first way is 'to relate ὅλος, πᾶς, ἅπαντες only to slaves—and the children postulated by Jeremias would be excluded' (A 90). But this course does not lead to its goal. For in the first place the texts say nothing about whether slaves belonged to the 'houses' mentioned. Thus there is room here for debate. Aland considers the existence of domestic slaves in the households mentioned in the New Testament to be 'virtually certain' (A 90); for myself, it seems to me to be open to question 'in view of the general socio-logical picture we have received of the oldest communities of the missionary church', whether 'the households of Cornelius, [or] of the keeper of the prison in Philippi . . . ever included a considerable group of slaves' (J 20). But even if this should have been the case, a second consideration arises against referring πᾶς, ὅλος, ἅπαντες, πανοικεί to slaves who might perhaps have been present. It would have to be assumed that at the conversion of the 'households' the whole domestic staff was regularly included in the conversion and the baptism. If we keep to the sources a different picture appears. Onesimus, the slave of the Christian Philemon, was converted by Paul only after his flight (Philemon 10, 16) and Aristides, *Apol.* 15.6, says that Christians 'encourage their slaves and maidservants to become Christians' and, when they have done so, they call them 'brothers without any kind of social discrimination (ἀμέριστοι ὄντες)'.[1] Here it is obviously not expected that all the servants were automatically baptized when their master was con-verted. And if allowance were made for this difficulty, too, even then there would remain a final compelling objection which Aland himself raises: 'On the other hand these slaves might have been married and had newly-born children' (A 90). Thus the restriction of πᾶς, ὅλος, etc., to the slaves does not help 'to exclude the children' from the οἶκος phrase.

So there remains only one other way of excluding the children from the New Testament statements about the conversion or bap-tism of complete households, namely the attempt to prove that in actual individual cases there could have been no intention of in-cluding them. Here it must be shown that the household in question contained no children or that what is said in the statement about the household can refer only to its adult members. Aland tries to adduce this double proof. It is true that from the outset this attempt is not very promising, since the sources say so little. Aland's exposition itself confirms this. Let us look at the individual passages.

'I did baptize also the household of Stephanas' (ἐβάπτισα δὲ καὶ τὸν Στεφανᾶ οἶκον, I Cor. 1.16), says the oldest of them. Now we

---

[1] On this passage see further, pp. 43ff. below.

read in I Cor. 16.15, about this οἰκία Στεφανᾶ, that it had laid itself out to lead the Corinthian community (so A 88, n. 1), or, rather, to collect the contributions for the Jerusalem church.[1]

According to Aland's argument the second passage enables us to see to what group of people the phrase 'the household of Stephanas' refers. 'That οἰκία = οἶκος in this passage relates only to adults needs no argument. With the best will in the world children cannot be included in this ministry of leading the church—to say nothing of infants!' (A 88, n. 1). This is quite true. Infants are not in the habit of collecting contributions! But it is a short circuit to conclude that since the statement in 16.15b refers only to the adult members of the οἰκία Στεφανᾶ, Στεφανᾶ οἶκος in 1.16 must have the same re-stricted group of persons in view, and that accordingly ἐβάπτισα δὲ καὶ τὸν Στεφανᾶ οἶκον would signify 'I baptized only the adult mem-bers of the house of Stephanas'. No readers of I Cor. 1.16 could understand the passage in this way, simply because nowhere in the whole of Hellenistic Greek literature nor in Jewish literature is οἶκος restricted to the adult members of the family. Nor, after all, is I Cor. 16.15 in actual fact any evidence for such a limiting usage. For here at the beginning of v. 15a the family as a whole is in mind (οἴδατε τὴν οἰκίαν Στεφανᾶ, ὅτι ἐστὶν ἀπαρχὴ τῆς Ἀχαΐας) and not until v. 15b with the transition to the third person plural is mention made of the efforts of its members to collect contributions (καὶ εἰς διακονίαν τοῖς ἁγίοις ἔταξαν ἑαυτούς). Therefore I Cor. 16.15 offers no support for the view that οἶκος in I Cor. 1.16 might have another and narrower meaning than the well-established one: the family, the household.[2]

'You will be saved and all your house' (σωθήσῃ σὺ καὶ πᾶς ὁ οἶκός σου), the angel says to Cornelius in Acts 11.14. Whom does this

---

[1] Such is, to my mind, the meaning of 'they made themselves available for the service of the holy ones' (εἰς διακονίαν τοῖς ἁγίοις ἔταξαν ἑαυτούς). Cf. II Cor. 8.4; 9.1: ἡ διακονία ἡ εἰς τοὺς ἁγίους; Rom. 15.25: διακονῶν τοῖς ἁγίοις; in addition 15.31 and, in our present context, I Cor. 16.1.

[2] Besides we should also ask whether Aland's assumption that οἶκος (I Cor. 1.16) and οἰκία (16.15) are completely synonymous is correct. In the Septuagint, it is true, these two words are occasionally found to overlap in meaning. This is connected with the fact that the Hebrew knows no differentiation corresponding to the Greek; but it is worth noting that these cases are rare. Secular Greek usage (e.g. the papyri) so far as I could ascertain shows different shades of meaning: οἶκος denotes the members of the household in its entirety, whilst οἰκία is used by preference when speaking of the reputation or social position of the family, of its internal or economic organization, or in a wider sense, of all the kin. The change in the word between I Cor. 1.16 (οἶκος) and 16.15 (οἰκία) fits in well with this: the first passage is concerned with the household in its entirety, the second with the family as a group of representative persons.

οἶκος comprise? Aland entertains the possibility that Cornelius was a bachelor ('if he had [a wife]', A 91). But this possibility is excluded in view of 10.2: He was 'religious and worshipped God with all his household' (εὐσεβὴς καὶ φοβούμενος τὸν θεὸν σὺν παντὶ τῷ οἴκῳ αὐτοῦ). For the statement that 'the whole οἶκος' belonged to the group of half-proselytes cannot refer to the slaves or to the orderlies (10.7) detailed for the personal service of an unmarried officer; on the contrary, in this passage, where the religious position of the 'house' is described, πᾶς ὁ οἶκος can denote only the whole family. The phrase in 11.14 must therefore be understood accordingly. Unfortunately we are not told of whom the family was composed.

It is said of Lydia (Acts 16.15) that 'she was baptized and all her household' (ἐβαπτίσθη καὶ ὁ οἶκος αὐτῆς). She behaves in an independent manner as the mistress of the house. Her οἶκος was therefore either 'that of an unmarried woman or of a widow', and therefore there belonged to it 'either no children at all, or at least there were no little children or infants' (A 89). 'Children or the very young or infants could be brought into this household only by way of appeal to the slaves who belonged to it' (A 90). Is the 'only' really correct? What if Lydia was a young widow? Or if she was an older one, which, in view of the offer of hospitality to the missionaries, is by far the most likely, and her house consisted of married children and their children?

In the account of the conversion of the jailer of Philippi we read in Acts 16.31–33: 'They said, "Trust in the Lord Jesus and you will be saved and all your household." And they spoke the word of God to him and to all who were in his house. . . . And he was baptized and all his people, instantly' (οἱ δὲ εἶπαν· πίστευσον ἐπὶ τὸν κύριον Ἰησοῦν, καὶ σωθήσῃ σὺ καὶ ὁ οἶκός σου. καὶ ἐλάλησαν αὐτῷ τὸν λόγον τοῦ θεοῦ σὺν πᾶσιν τοῖς ἐν τῇ οἰκίᾳ αὐτοῦ . . . καὶ ἐβαπτίσθη αὐτὸς καὶ οἱ αὐτοῦ ἅπαντες παραχρῆμα). 'The report in 16.32, that the jailer received baptismal instruction "with all who were in his house", does not exactly demand the assumption that infants were included in these πᾶσιν' (A 91). But it would be pedantic to expect an addition such as: 'the youngest child was brought in half asleep at the end of the instruction for baptism' or 'even the smallest was present, though it was too young to understand anything'. In any case it is certain that no less than three times it is emphasized that the family was complete. The preceding paratactic formula 'you and your household' (σὺ καὶ ὁ οἶκός σου, v. 31), which will occupy us later, reappears in three different forms: in v. 32 (αὐτῷ σὺν πᾶσιν τοῖς ἐν τῇ οἰκίᾳ αὐτοῦ), in v. 33 (αὐτὸς καὶ οἱ αὐτοῦ ἅπαντες), in v. 34 (πανοικεί).

'Crispus, the Synagogue officer, became a believer in the Lord along with all his household' (Κρίσπος δὲ ὁ ἀρχισυνάγωγος ἐπίστευσεν τῷ κυρίῳ σὺν ὅλῳ τῷ οἴκῳ αὐτοῦ, Acts 18.8). Yet Paul says in I Cor. 1.14 that he had baptized Crispus alone, without mentioning his house! 'What are we to make of this?' (A 88). Aland himself considers several possibilities. After all, it is not absolutely necessary to reconcile these passages. The account of Crispus' baptism might have been elaborated in the Acts; in that case Acts 18.8 would still remain an example of the use of the phrase 'he and his house' in the Lucan period. Or Paul might have expressed himself carelessly. Or he might have left the baptism of the rest of the family to assistants (cf. Acts 10.48; John 4.2), perhaps because the *oikos* of Crispus—this would not be so very far-fetched—had only female members (cf. *Gerim* 2.8: 'the baptism of a man is performed by a man, that of a woman by a woman'). But here we have reached guesswork.

Enough has been said! In no single case does the New Testament—alas!—tell us more precisely of whom the 'houses' embracing the Christian faith were composed; nor in any single case can children be excluded from belonging to the house. In no instance is it possible to limit with Aland the idea of the *oikos* in any New Testament passage to its adult members, because, as we shall see, there is no evidence of this restrictive use of *oikos* either in secular Greek or in biblical Greek or the writings of Hellenistic Judaism.

2. 'HE AND HIS HOUSE'

We begin to stand on firmer ground when we cease to consider the individual passages of the New Testament and turn to the linguistic usage of 'house' in the sense of the 'family'. On pp. 19–24 of my book I had deduced from a double set of facts that in the New Testament passages concerning the salvation, conversion or baptism of a house the children of every age must be included, firstly because, as already noted, οἶκος can be supplemented by πᾶς, ὅλος or replaced by οἱ αὐτοῦ ἅπαντες, πανοικεί; secondly because in several passages the customary formula 'he and his (whole) house' is found, which in the Old Testament usage, according to an investigation by E. Stauffer,[1] includes the children, in fact has them particularly in view.

[1] 'Zur Kindertaufe in der Urkirche', *Deutsches Pfarrerblatt* 49, 1949, 152–4.

Aland has evidently not recognized the form-critical approach in the observations of Stauffer and myself; therefore he refutes them (apart from the attempt already discussed to eliminate children on historical grounds from the 'houses' baptized according to the evidence of the New Testament) by merely counting up the number of times each of the lexical senses of οἶκος is used in the New Testament (A 87f.); this shows him that the nine (I reckon at least twelve)[1] passages in which the word has the figurative sense of 'family' are few in comparison with the total number of examples. It is not clear what this reference to the relatively small number of passages in the New Testament (and similarly in the LXX) in which οἶκος denotes 'family' is intended to signify. It can, after all, make absolutely no difference to the range of meaning of *oikos*/family, and particularly to the phrase 'he and his house', that beside the twelve examples of this shade of meaning there are sixty others in which οἶκος indicates a building. Evidently Aland supposes that the smaller number of examples of οἶκος/family leaves the sense of this nuance so vague that nothing can be inferred from it with regard to children. Furthermore, he asserts that the New Testament turn of speech conforms completely to the secular Greek usage: 'In the usage of οἶκος with which we are concerned we have to do with a linguistic phenomenon that runs completely parallel to the profane (since Homer!) and that is not to be distinguished from it' (A 92). What do the sources tell us?

Let us begin with the *secular Greek usage*. Examples of οἶκος meaning family are found in classical Greek, though perhaps not as early as in Homer, as Aland states.[2] But in Hesiod, Pindar, Plato and the tragic poets[3] examples are found which become more numerous in the ensuing period. These show unambiguously that οἶκος denotes the family including the children; and the papyri confirm this range of meaning by the fact that οἶκος alternates with πανοικεί and πανοικία.[4] On the other hand I have not found in

---

[1] Aland admits only: I Cor. 1.16; Acts 10.2; 11.14; 16.15, 31; 18.8; II Tim. 1.16; 4.19; Titus 1.11. To these must be added: Luke 10.5 (note the change from οἰκία to οἶκος); 19.9; Heb. 11.7. Beside these Arndt and Gingrich *s.v.* include here also I Tim. 3.4, 5, 12; 5.4; Heb. 3.6b.

[2] In the relevant passages in Homer οἶκος does not refer with special emphasis to the persons composing the household, but rather to the household goods, the property cf. *Od.* 2.48, 64, 226; 4.318; 6.181; 7.314; 16.431; *Il.* 15.498.

[3] H. Stephanus, *Thesaurus Graecae Linguae*[3] V, Paris, 1842–6, col. 1796f.

[4] Cf. F. Preisigke, *Wörterbuch der griechischen Papyrusurkunden* II, Berlin, 1927, col. 162 *s.v.* οἶκος with col. 227 *s.v.* πανοικεί, πανοικία.

secular Greek usage any examples of οἶκος referring to 'adults exclusively' (A 93).

As regards phrases of the type 'N.N. and his house' no literary examples are found in the dictionaries in general use; in non-literary language it occurs, at any rate in Egypt, only in two specific types of religious inscriptions and here and there in the epistolary style.[1] In the case of the inscriptions there are, first, dedications in honour of the emperor which, with insignificant variations, employ the stereotyped phrase 'for . . .' (then follows the name with titles, possibly the co-emperor and the emperor's relations) 'and his house' (ὑπέρ . . . καὶ τοῦ οἴκου αὐτοῦ).[2] Secondly, we find votive inscriptions of people who have said their prayers in the temple (*proskynemata*), and on these there occurs frequently the phrase 'Act of worship of N.N. (also perhaps of his wife and the members of the family) and of his house' (τὸ προσκύνημα . . . καὶ τοῦ οἴκου αὐτοῦ).[3] However, the usage of the inscriptions differs from that of the New Testament and also from that of the Old Testament which will shortly be discussed. For not infrequently in the dedicatory inscriptions and generally in the *proskynemata* the wording contains a series of names ending up with οἶκος, instead of the two parts 'N.N. and his house'. Moreover women are often mentioned in the *proskynemata*, for example, the wife (σύμβιος), beside the father of the family. In addition to the inscriptions the phrase 'N.N. and his house' appears in the greetings formulae of letters,[4] but only in isolated examples. It is on the whole usual for the hypotactic form with σύν or μετά to be employed in place of the paratactic one with

[1] I rely on the larger corpora of papyri and above all on F. Preisigke's *Sammelbuch* and his dictionary: F. Preisigke, *Sammelbuch Griechischer Urkunden aus Aegypten* I, Strassburg, 1915; II, Berlin–Leipzig, 1922; F. Bilabel, III, Berlin–Leipzig, 1927; IV, Heidelberg, 1931; F. Bilabel–E. Kiessling, V, Wiesbaden, 1955 (referred to hereafter as *SB*); Preisigke, *Wörterbuch der griechischen Papyrusurkunden* II, col. 156f. (οἰκία); 161–3 (οἶκος). The supplement has not yet reached the letter ὀ.

[2] *SB* I, 85, No. 999 (Koptos, AD 105): Ὑπὲρ Αὐτοκράτορος Καίσαρος Νέρουα Τραιανοῦ Σεβαστοῦ Γερμανικοῦ Δακικοῦ καὶ τοῦ παντὸς οἴκου αὐτοῦ Ἴσιδι τῇ χώματος θεᾷ μεγίστῃ Βάλβιλλος Ἡρακλείδου ἀνέθηκεν ἐπ' ἀγαθῷ. Ἔτους θ΄. Παχὼν κγ. Similarly 24f., No. 305; 135, No. 1566; 300, No. 4227; 343, No. 4383; 622f., No. 5689; 638, No. 5802; *SB* V, 239, No. 8311; 239f., No. 8312; 240, No. 8317; 241, No. 8320; 242, Nos. 8324, 8325; 253f., No. 8386; 268, No. 8443; 332, No. 8815; 334f., No. 8830; 335, No. 8832; 355, No. 8905; 356f., No. 8912.

[3] *SB* I, 392, No. 4613 (Talmis [Kalabshah]): Τὸ προσκύνημα Ἀντ[ω]νίου Κλήμεντος ρ̄ καὶ τοῦ παντὸς αὐτοῦ οἴκου καὶ τοῦ γράψαντο[ς] παρὰ τῷ [κ]υρί[ῳ] Μανδούλι [- - -]; *SB* V, 278, No. 8481; 280, Nos. 8493, 8498; 303f., No. 8662; 306, No. 8681.

[4] *P. Oxy.*, 1299. 15, *P. Tebt.*, 413. 16–18; Princeton University, Garrett Dep. 7686. 14–17 (E. H. Kase jnr., *Papyri in the Princeton University Collections* II, Princeton, N.J., 1936, 71, No. 73).

καί.[1] It is most unlikely that the New Testament should have been influenced by a usage which is virtually confined to inscriptions, is clearly not idiomatic Greek[2] according to the evidence of the epistolary formulae, and is not even formally appropriate. Thus the secular Greek usage gives us no help. But the Old Testament certainly takes us further.

The *Old Testament*, too, employs 'house' (*bayit*) in the sense of 'family'. But the picture here is completely different from that in secular Greek. Aland has not noticed that *bayit*/family is used in the Old Testament almost always as part of a stereotyped formula. The examples fall into five definite phrases:

1. The house of N.N.[3]—frequent.

2. The whole house of N.N.—repeatedly (add to this seventeen examples under No. 5).

3. To make (build) a house—Ex. 1.21; Deut. 25.9; II Sam. 7.11, 27; I Kings 2.24; 11.38; Prov. 24.27; Ruth 4.11.

4. *Y*ᵉ*lid bayit* of the slave born in the household—Gen. 14.14; 17.12f., 23, 27; Lev. 22.11; Jer. 2.14.

5. He and his (whole) house—frequently.

The following classification of the examples in this fifth group gives us in each case the variations and amplifications under the basic form, e.g. 'he, his sons and his whole house' is listed under 'he and his house'. (* indicates that 'whole' (*kol*) is added.)

(*a*) I and my house—Gen. 34.30; Josh. 24.15.

Thou and thy (whole) house—Gen. 7.1*; 45.11; Deut. 14.26; 15.20; 26.11; Judg. 18.25; I Sam. 25.6; II Kings 8.1; Jer. 38.17.

He and his (whole) house—Gen. 12.17; 18.19; 36.6*; 45.8*; 50.7f.*; Ex. 1.1; Lev. 16.6, 11, 17; Deut. 6.22*; I Sam. 1.21*; 27.3; II Sam. 2.3; 6.11*, 21*; 9.9*; 15.16*; 19.42; 21.1, 4; I Kings 16.7.

She and her house—II Kings 8.2.

You and your houses—Gen. 45.18; Num. 18.31; Deut. 12.7.

---

[1] *SB* III, 252f., No. 7242. 24f. (a papyrus letter, end of the 2nd century AD, origin unknown): Ἐρρῶσθαί σε εὔχομαι πανοικὶ μετὰ τοῦ οἴκου σου ὅλου, ἄδελφε Ἀπίω[ν]; *P. Oxy.*, 2273, fr. B 24–26; *P. Hamb.*, 54.32; *P. Soc.*, 236.38; cf. also Ign. *Pol.*, 8.2. Besides 'N.N. with his house' occurs also in *proskynemata* parallel with the form having 'and', cf. *SB* I, 102, No. 1155; V, 140, No. 7912.

[2] This will be confirmed below from Philo and Josephus (see below, pp. 20f.).

[3] *bet 'ab* (father's house) and *bet 'abot* (family, tribe race) are included under 1.

(b) I and the (whole) house of my father—Gen. 46.31b; I Sam. 22.15*; II Sam. 14.9; I Kings 2.31; Neh. 1.6.

Thou and the (whole) house of thy father—Num. 18.1; Josh. 2.18*; Judg. 14.15; I Sam. 2.30, 31; 9.20*; 22.16*; I Kings 18.18; Esth. 4.14; Isa. 7.17; Jer. 12.6.

He and the (whole) house of his father—Gen. 46.31a; 47.12*; 50.8, 22; Judg. 16.31*; I Sam. 22.1*.

She and the house of her father—Josh. 6.25; Judg. 15.6.

This survey of the passages in which *bayit* occurs in the Old Testament in the sense of 'family' yields the following result: If we disregard the simplest form, 'house of N.N.' (or 'house' with suffixes), *bayit*/family occurs almost solely in definite phrases and, in fact, the *overwhelming majority* of the examples consist of the phrase 'he and his house' with variations (5). This phrase corresponds to the Semitic manner of thinking and speaking, as regards its content (with its emphasis on the authority of the father of the family and the omission of the mother of the family) as well as regards its form (with its parataxis). E. Stauffer coined for it the term the '*oikos* formula'.[1] His conjecture that we have here a 'ritual formula', in particular one taken from the terminology of circumcision,[2] is not indeed confirmed by the sources, as Aland (A 92f.) has correctly observed.[3] On the contrary the phrase is distributed widely both in secular and in cultic contexts. For this reason I should prefer to speak no longer of the '*oikos* formula', but of the '*oikos* phrase'.

The phrase 'he and his house' (5) lives on in the *period between the Testaments*. It is attested for the sphere of Palestinian Judaism by Jub. 15.24*; 23.6*; 1 Q Gen Ap 20.15*, 16*, 17*, 18*, 19f., 28*; 21.21*.[4] The Septuagint made it familiar to Hellenistic Judaism; it was also employed in the Apocrypha (I Macc. 1.6of.; 2.18A; 13.3; 14.26; 16.2; Ps. Sol. 3.8; Bel and the Dragon 29Θ); it is found, too, in the Hexaplaric translations (Jer. 12.6Σ; 38[45].17'ΑΣ). But it is absent from Philo and Josephus, who, when reproducing Old Testament narratives, replace it with πανοικ(ε)ί.[5] This shows

[1] 'Zur Kindertaufe in der Urkirche', *Deutsches Pfarrerblatt* 49, 1949, 152–4; I followed him in this (J 19–24).
[2] *Op. cit.*, 153.
[3] The only example of a connexion with circumcision is in Jub. 15.24: 'Abraham was circumcised and all the people of his house.'
[4] * indicates that *kol* is added.
[5] Philo, *De Josepho* 251; *De Vita Mos.* I, 5; Josephus, *Ant.* 4.70, 300; 5.11.

that the phrase was not used by Hellenistic Jewry in literary language, but was felt to be a biblicism. However, as such it was in full and active use.

In the *New Testament* we find the phrase 'he and his house'

(a) in the paratactic form—John 4.53 (with οἰκία)*; Acts 11.14*; 16.15, 31, cf. 33 (αὐτὸς καὶ οἱ αὐτοῦ ἅπαντες)*;

(b) grecianized by σύν instead of καί—Acts 10.2*; 16.32 (with οἰκία)*; 18.8*;

by πανοικεί—16.34*.[1]

In view of the dissimilarities of the New Testament phrase 'he and his house' to secular Greek (see above pp. 18f.) and its agreement with the Old Testament and LXX usage there can be no doubt that it represents a heritage from biblical language. Since all the examples except John 4.53 occur in the Acts, and as Luke in other cases, too, is fond of using biblical expressions, we may ask whether it was Luke who introduced this phrase into primitive Christian usage. However, this question must certainly be answered in the negative, since the phrase is used, independently of Luke, in its old paratactic form in St John's Gospel (4.53), in I *Clement* (12.5; a free composition, not copying the LXX of Josh. 2.12f.) and in Hermas.[2] It was, in fact, also current in the early Church outside the sphere of Lucan influence as well. It cannot be proved that we are concerned here with a usage 'that runs completely parallel to the profane (since Homer!) and that is not to be distinguished from it' (A 92). If Aland maintains this, the explanation is, as he admits, that he has dispensed with 'a detailed investigation' (A 92f.). He should not be in any way blamed for this (it is a very laborious task to sift the material, since the total number of occurrences of *bayit/oὶκος* and οἰκία is very large). But if this has been left undone, greater care should be exercised in expressing an opinion.

What group of people does the phrase 'He and his house' have in view? That is the vital question. The answer is as follows. In the Old Testament it denotes the *complete family* and in many cases the inclusiveness is emphasized by the addition of *kol*. Together with

---

[1] The asterisk indicates the addition of πᾶς, ὅλος or the paraphrase ἅπαντες.

[2] 'Thou and thy (whole) house': *Vis.* I, 1.9*; *Mand.* II, 7; V, 1.7; *Sim.* VII, 5. 'Thou and thy children and thy (whole) house': *Mand.* XII, 3.6; *Sim.* V, 3.9* (σὺ μετὰ . . .); VII, 6 (asterisk = addition of ὅλος).—From the next period cf. *Epistula Abgari* 2 (R. A. Lipsius and M. Bonnet, *Acta Apostolorum Apocrypha* I, Leipzig, 1891, p. 281, ll. 3f.); *Act. Phil.* 66, 69 (*op. cit.*, II, 2, Leipzig, 1903, pp. 27, ll. 20f.; 28.6).

'his (whole) house' the father of the family eats a meal;[1] he changes
his dwelling-place 'with all the persons' and 'all the property';[2] 'he
and his household' seek a refuge,[3] are blessed,[4] saved,[5] stricken with
plagues,[6] annihilated,[7] burned,[8] killed[9]—all these things are done or
suffered by all members of the family without exception. 'The
house' together with the father of the family serves the Lord as a
cultic community[10] and goes up to offer sacrifice;[11] all its male
members are circumcised;[12] 'his house after him' is the designation
of one's descendants.[13] A distinction is made between a man's own
house and 'his father's house',[14] the large family; the large family of
Jacob numbered seventy persons.[15] The sons represent the house
besides their father;[16] hence within the framework of the levirate
regulations 'to build up one's brother's house' means to beget a son
for him (Deut. 25.9). Accordingly the large family consisted of the
father of the family, the married sons and 'the whole (the rest of the)
house'.[17]

Whoever takes the trouble to check the examples in their context
will confirm the fact that repeatedly the presence of children and
infants is specially mentioned,[18] and at times their omission is
particularly emphasized.[19] What is more, Stauffer's conclusion was
by no means formulated in 'the heat of combat' (A 93), but was
based on a careful analysis when he stated that 'not simply the
children in addition to the adults, but the children *quite especially*,
and not least any *little children* who might be present' were in view.[20]
The families consist of the father of the family, the mother of the
family, the sons and the *taph*,[21] that is to say, of men, women
and *taph*,[22] and in this connexion *taph* denoted originally those
members of a nomadic tribe who were not able to march, i.e.
the infants and the old people; later on only the children. The

[1] Deut. 12.7; 14.26; 15.20; also Num. 18.31.
[2] Gen. 36.6; cf. Ex. 1.1; II Sam. 2.3; 15.16.
[3] Gen. 7.1; I Sam. 27.3.   [4] I Sam. 25.6; II Sam. 6.11.   [5] Jer. 38.17.   [6] Gen. 12.17.
[7] Gen. 34.30; Judg. 18.25; Esth. 4.14.   [8] Judg. 14.15.   [9] Bel and the Dragon, 29 Θ.
[10] Josh. 24.15.   [11] I Sam. 1.21.   [12] Gen. 17.23.   [13] Gen. 18.19; cf. I Sam. 2.30.
[14] For examples see p. 20 above.   [15] Gen. 46.27.   [16] I Chron. 10.6.
[17] Hence the triad 'You and your sons and your father's house' in Num. 18.1; 'he, his
brothers and his father's house' in Gen. 46.31; 47.12; Judg. 16.31; I Sam. 22.1.
[18] Cf. Gen. 46.27 with vv. 5, 7; I Sam. 22.15f. with v. 19; II Kings 9.8; Jer. 38.17
with v. 23.
[19] Gen. 50.8; I Sam. 1.21f.; cf. Ex. 12.37.
[20] *Op. cit.*, 153 (Stauffer's italics).   [21] Num. 16.27; II Chron. 20.13.
[22] Gen. 34.25–29; Num. 14.1–3; 31.7–9; 32.26f.; Deut. 2.34; 3.6; 31.12; Josh. 1.14;
8.35; Judg. 21.10; Esth. 3.13; 8.11; Jer. 40.7; 41.16; 43.6.

male and female slaves can be considered as part of the 'house';[1] but often the subject-matter or the context excludes the possibility that the slaves were reckoned in.[2] If it is intended to express with particular force that an occurrence affected every member of the house, it is habitually described by saying that the *taph*, too, indeed even the infants, are included. All the male members of the house are circumcised—down to the infant eight days old (Gen. 17.12, 23). The father's house emigrates, women and *taph* in wagons (45.19; 46.5, 7). A hungry house receives food—according to the number of the *taph* (47.12). 'Four fifths shall be your own as seed for the field and as food for all who are in your households and as food for your *taph*' (47.24). The whole father's house is destroyed down to 'children and sucklings' (I Sam. 22.15f., 19).[3] The whole congregation is to assemble—even children and nursing infants (Joel 2.16). Finally *taph* or *'olalim* (children) can occur, as the most defenceless part of the family, simply as a short name for 'the whole house'. '. . . that we may not die, both we and you and our *taph*' (Gen. 43.8). 'I will provide for you and your *taph*' (50.21). Those who bear arms march out—the *taph* remains behind in the fortified cities (Num. 32.17; cf. 16.24). Jerusalem's 'children' have gone into captivity (Lam. 1.5). Those who return pray for a good journey for themselves and their *taph* (Ezra 8.21). Whilst children can represent the 'house', there is no passage in the Old Testament in which the term *bayit* = family is restricted to its adult male and female members.[4]

The Septuagint as well as Aquila and Symmachus usually give a literal rendering of the *oikos* phrase of the Hebrew original. But the translators did not do so merely mechanically; they had a lively sense of the meaning of the 'complete family'. This is shown by several passages in which (sometimes as the translation of *bayit*, sometimes

---

[1] Cf., e.g. Deut. 14.26: 'Rejoice, you and your household' with 12.12: 'you shall rejoice before the Lord your God, you and your sons and your daughters, your men servants and your maidservants.'

[2] E.g. Num. 18.1; I Sam. 2.30; 9.20; II Sam. 9.9; *et al.*

[3] Cf. Deut. 2.34; 3.6; 32.25; Judg. 21.10; I Sam. 15.3; Esth. 3.13; 8.11; Jer. 44.7; Hos. 13.16.

[4] Gen. 7.1 ('Go into the ark, you and all your house') is no proof of the opposite. It is true that in this particular case the 'whole *oikos*' was composed only of adults, viz. Noah, his wife, his three sons and their wives (Gen. 7.13), at least according to the interpretation current in NT times (cf. I Peter 3.20, 'eight souls'). But this does not mean that 'house' is used here in a narrower sense for its adult members only; in Gen. 7.1, as everywhere else in the OT, it stands for the complete family, a family which, in this particular instance, lacked little children.

without a word in the original) the expression πανοικία,[1] twice intensified to πᾶσα ἡ πανοικία,[2] is employed. In two other passages, moreover, the Hebrew *taph* is rendered by 'house' (Gen. 50.21 LXX: τὰς οἰκίας ὑμῶν; Judg. 18.21 LXX 'A: τὴν πανοικίαν [also Θ]); hence the translators—hitting the nail pertinently on the head in both passages—regarded the young children as the designation *pars pro toto* for the complete family.

Finally if we ask what persons the *oikos* phrase covered in the early Christian writings, the only detail supplied by the New Testament is that the 'whole house' mentioned in John 4.53 contained a παιδίον (v. 49). Hermas, who often uses the phrase (twice with the addition of ὅλος),[3] gives us the fullest information. From *Vis.* II, 2.3; 3.1 we learn that his 'house' consists of his wife and his children;[4] and Ignatius confirms that this is the usual meaning.[5] In *Vis.* I, 3.1 (at the beginning) the term is restricted to the children, as it is already occasionally in the Old Testament ('your house who wronged the Lord and you, their parents'),[6] and the immediate continuation agrees with this ('loving your children you did not admonish your house').[7]

The picture is always the same. The phrase 'he and his (whole) house' denotes the complete family; normally husband, wife and children. In no single case is the term 'house' restricted to the adult members of the house, though on the other hand children alone may be mentioned when the whole house is meant. Whilst the slaves are very often not reckoned as part of the 'house', the inclusion of the children is taken for granted. Indeed, the Old Testament repeatedly lays special emphasis on the very smallest being reckoned in. Since the primitive Church takes the phrase over as a firmly established biblical expression, the statement 'it includes small children as well as others' (J 21) applies to its employment in the New Testament as well. This appears to Aland to be 'greatly exaggerated, and not alone with respect to the circle of people involved' (A 92). I must confess that this sentence is totally incomprehensible to me. In what way

---

[1] LXX Ex. 1.1; Esth. 8.12r; III Macc. 3.27. [2] LXX Gen. 50.8, 22.
[3] See above, p. 21.
[4] It is of no consequence for our inquiry whether Hermas' 'house' was an actual or a fictitious one.
[5] *Smyrn.* 13.1: 'I send greetings to the houses of my brothers with [their] wives and children' (ἀσπάζομαι τοὺς οἴκους τῶν ἀδελφῶν μου σὺν γυναιξὶ καὶ τέκνοις).
[6] τὸν οἶκόν σου τὸν ἀνομήσαντα εἰς τὸν κύριον καὶ εἰς ὑμᾶς τοὺς γονεῖς αὐτῶν.
[7] φιλότεκνος ὢν οὐκ ἐνουθέτεις σου τὸν οἶκον.

should it be 'exaggerated', indeed 'greatly exaggerated', to establish the fact (which is, after all, already expressed, even without the wealth of examples, by the plain straightforward words) that the phrase 'he and his whole house' includes the small children? Are we speaking different languages?

3. THE BAPTISM OF 'HOUSES'

Only now can we begin to speak of baptism. The baptism of a 'house' is expressly mentioned in I Cor. 1.16 (Stephanas) and in Acts 16.15 (Lydia). Acts 16.33 also belongs here: 'He [the jailer of Philippi] was baptized and all his people' (ἐβαπτίσθη αὐτὸς καὶ οἱ αὐτοῦ ἅπαντες). But in 11.14, too, 'You [Cornelius] will be saved and all your household' (σωθήσῃ σὺ καὶ πᾶς ὁ οἶκός σου), the baptism of the house is implied; for the sentence occurs again in 16.31[1] and is explained there by vv. 32–34. The same holds good for 18.8 (Crispus), where v. 8a ('he became a believer in the Lord along with all his household', ἐπίστευσεν τῷ κυρίῳ σὺν ὅλῳ τῷ οἴκῳ αὐτοῦ), is explained more fully by the continuation in v. 8b ('and many Corinthians who had listened became believers and were baptized', καὶ πολλοὶ τῶν Κορινθίων ἀκούοντες ἐπίστευον καὶ ἐβαπτίζοντο). In all five cases the linguistic evidence forbids us to restrict the concept of the 'house' to the adult members of the family. On the contrary it shows plainly that it is *the complete family including all its members* which receives baptism.

Acts 2.38f. belongs here as well: 'Be baptized, every one of you, . . . and you shall receive the gift of the Holy Spirit. (39) For the promise is to you and to your children and to all those who are far away, whom the Lord our God may call' (βαπτίσθητω ἕκαστος ὑμῶν . . . καὶ λήμψεσθε τὴν δωρεὰν τοῦ ἁγίου πνεύματος. (39) ὑμῖν γάρ ἐστιν ἡ ἐπαγγελία καὶ τοῖς τέκνοις ὑμῶν καὶ πᾶσιν τοῖς εἰς μακράν, ὅσους ἂν προσκαλέσηται κύριος ὁ θεὸς ἡμῶν). Verse 38 promises to those who will let themselves be baptized that they will receive the Spirit and v. 39 adds that this promise applies 'to you and to your children and to all those who are far away' (πᾶσιν τοῖς εἰς μακράν). Who is meant by this triad in v. 39? Aland, who by the way gives a quite grotesquely wrong interpretation of my ideas of this passage,[2]

---

[1] Only πᾶς is missing here. Yet there follows in v. 32 σὺν πᾶσιν, in v. 33 ἅπαντες, and in v. 34 πανοικεί.

[2] As contrasted with 'not a few exegetes' (A 84, n. 5) I am supposed to consider Peter's speech, 'as reproduced in the Acts of the Apostles', to be historical (A 84)!

replies that the triad means (*a*) the adult listeners (ὑμῖν), (*b*) their descendants (τοῖς τέκνοις ὑμῶν), and (*c*) the coming generations (πᾶσιν τοῖς εἰς μακράν) (A 86). Thus there would be no mention in Acts 2.39 of children in the proper sense of the word, but only of descendants, and the passage would have nothing to do with our subject. However, this exegesis of Acts 2.39 will not stand up to examination. (1) We will begin with the third member (καὶ πᾶσιν τοῖς εἰς μακράν). The 'promise' of God, the subject of v. 39, is the outpouring of the Spirit quoted from Joel 2.28–32 (Hebrew 3.1–5a) = Acts 2.17–21, and the triad in v. 39 paraphrases the recipients of the Spirit's gift described there. This applies also to the third term of the triad: 'and all who are far away, whom the Lord, our God, may call' (καὶ πᾶσιν τοῖς εἰς μακράν, ὅσους ἂν προσκαλέσηται κύριος ὁ θεὸς ἡμῶν), for it must be observed that the second part of Joel 2.32 (Heb. 3.5b), 'for on Mount Zion and in Jerusalem there will be such as are saved, as the Lord said, and as are told the good news, whom the Lord has called' (ὅτι ἐν τῷ ὄρει Σιων καὶ ἐν Ιερουσαλημ ἔσται ἀνασῳζόμενος, καθότι εἶπεν κύριος, καὶ εὐαγγελιζόμενοι, οὓς κύριος προσκέκληται), is not included in the citation in Acts 2.17–21, but is actually taken into account in v. 39. This can be gathered from the fact that the subordinate clause at the end of v. 39 (ὅσους ἂν προσ- καλέσηται κύριος ὁ θεὸς ἡμῶν) is taken from Joel 2.32b (οὓς κύριος προσκέκληται). Now, in Joel 2.32b we have the picture, occurring so often in the Old and New Testaments, of the eschatological pil- grimage to Mount Zion,[1] and the continuation of Joel's text con- firms this. That is to say, the word 'far' (μακράν) in the third part of the triad in Acts 2.39 quite certainly signifies distance not in time (A 86) but in space, and the phrase 'those who are far away' (οἱ εἰς μακράν [sc. ὄντες]) does not refer to 'coming generations' (A 86) but to all those whom God summons from distant lands, i.e. according to the Lucan point of view, the Gentiles (cf. Acts 22.21: εἰς ἔθνη μακράν). (2) As regards the first two terms of the triad in Acts 2.39 (ὑμῖν . . . καὶ τοῖς τέκνοις ὑμῶν), they can be understood only if we do not tear them apart, because we have here a stereotyped formula which often recurs in the Old Testament. The phrase 'you and your children' with its variants (I and my children, thou and thy children, etc.) is a formula on the same lines as 'you and your houses', which has already been discussed; it is a biblical expression like the latter

---

[1] Cf. J. Jeremias, *Jesus' Promise to theNations*, ET, London, 1958, 57ff.

and often alternates with it.[1] Both phrases express completeness and both admit of no restriction. In its context 'you and your children' (2.29) reproduces the list in 2.17 (= Joel 2.28 [Heb. 3.1]), 'your sons and your daughters, your young men and your old men', which is likewise a paraphrase for the family in its completeness. Verse 39 declares that the promise of the Spirit is complete and unlimited; it comprises the 'houses' of Israel as well as the Gentiles. Thus our passage, too, belongs with the other statements in the Acts about the 'houses' which have already been discussed. It is true that baptism is not expressly mentioned in v. 39, but it is implied inasmuch as the fulfilment of the promise of the Spirit is linked in v. 38 with baptism.

Our conclusion that the complete families were baptized is confirmed by the analogy of the procedure in proselyte baptism. The contacts between primitive Christian baptism and proselyte baptism, as regards both the baptismal terminology and the baptismal rite with its interpretation and its symbols, go back to the early days of the Church; for Jewish proselytizing, and accordingly proselyte baptism, practically came to an end when Hadrian imposed the death penalty for circumcision shortly before AD 132.[2] These contacts are so numerous and so detailed (J 24–40) that they cannot be simply thrust aside. Nor can the significance of these agreements between the Christian and the Jewish baptismal rites be reduced by pointing out that the influences of Palestinian Jewish Christianity declined to a remarkable extent even in the first century (A 83f.), for, in the first place, particularly in the case of rites, it is the initial period which, in fact, matters most of all; and secondly the tenacious survival of what was taken over as a liturgical inheritance from the practice of proselyte baptism can be demonstrated. A far-reaching correspondence, extending down to particular rules, exists between the administration of the two rites (to take, for instance, the regulation that before baptism women should loosen their hair and lay aside their ornaments, which was originally intended to prevent the hair and the ornaments from bringing about a 'separation' or

---

[1] Compare, e.g., Gen. 45.11 MT 'Thou and thy house' with the LXX 'Thou and thy sons' (σὺ καὶ οἱ υἱοί σου); Esth. 8.12r 'because he himself . . . was crucified along with all his family' (διὰ τὸ αὐτὸν . . . ἐσταυρῶσθαι σὺν τῇ πανοικίᾳ) with 9.25 'he was himself hanged and his children' (ἐκρεμάσθη αὐτὸς καὶ τὰ τέκνα αὐτοῦ); in I Macc. 2.18A 'you and your house' (σὺ καὶ ὁ οἶκός σου) alternates with 'you and your sons' (σὺ καὶ οἱ υἱοί σου).

[2] Jeremias, op. cit., 9.

'dissociation' [*ḥaṣiṣa*] between the body and the water which would nullify the effect of the cleansing).[1] In view of this correspondence there is every probability that with regard to children, too, the primitive Christian practice in baptism followed that of proselyte baptism, in which all children, including infants, were baptized with the others.

We actually possess indirect evidence for the fact that the baptism of the 'whole house' included the children. The Pseudo-Clementine writings constantly repeat the rule that a Christian may under no circumstances sit at table with a pagan; this holds good even for father, mother, wife, child, brother and other relations.[2] As it is completely out of the question that the table-fellowship of families should be destroyed, the rule presupposes that when a pagan household was baptized, all the members of the family were included. The passages concerned occur in the *Homilies* as well as in the *Recognitions* and are therefore to be attributed to the *earliest version* which came into existence about AD 220–230 in Western Syria.[3] But we are brought into a much earlier period by the observation that the rule goes back[4] to the Jewish prohibition of sitting at table with pagans.[5] This relationship makes it extremely probable that the rule originated in the early days of Jewish Christianity.

What happened at the baptism of 'houses', at any rate in 215–20, we learn from Hippolytus' *Apostolic Tradition* (21.4f.). First the examination of the catechumens before their admission, their three years' catechumenate and their preparation for baptism during the days immediately preceding the ceremony are described at length.[6] Then the section concerning the baptism itself begins with the words: 'At cock-crow let prayers first be said over the water' (21.1). From this indication of time we must infer that Hippolytus has in mind the great festival of baptism on Easter morning (after the

---

[1] *Miqwaot* 9.1; *b. Baba Qamma* 82 ab. Christian: Hippolytus, *Apostolic Tradition* 21.5 (cited according to the numeration of G. Dix's translation, London, 1937); cf. W. C. van Unnik, 'Les cheveux défaits des femmes baptisées. Un rite de baptême dans l'*Ordre Ecclésiastique d'Hippolyte*', *Vigiliae Christianae* 1, 1947, 77–100.

[2] *Hom.* 13.4.4; 13.8.4; 13.9.1f.; 13.11.3f.; 14.1.4; 15.1.2, and the parallels in *Rec.* 7.29ff.; 10.1ff.

[3] For this dating cf. B. Rehm, *Die Pseudoklementinen I : Homilien* (GCS 42), 1953, VII.

[4] Cf. E. Molland, 'La circoncision, le baptême et l'autorité du décret apostolique (Actes XV, 28 sq.) dans les milieux judéo-chrétiens des Pseudo-Clémentines', *Studia Theologica* 9, 1955, 1–39, here 24.

[5] Str. Bill. IV, 353–414, especially 374–8.

[6] *Apostolic Tradition* 16–20.

conclusion of the Easter vigil at cock-crow). In North Africa, too, it was customary in 220 to admit the catechumens into the Church on Easter morning: 'Easter is the day preferred for baptism' (*diem baptismo sollemniorem pascha praestat*), says Tertullian.[1] The baptism itself followed in three groups: 'First you should baptize the little ones. All who can speak for themselves, should speak. But for those who cannot speak, their parents should speak, or another who belongs to their family. Then baptize the grown men, lastly the women.'[2] When we consider that the preceding passage deals with the catechumens and their three years' probationary period, that moreover amongst the adults catechumens are not only 'present' (A 52), but that they are the only people concerned (because there is no evidence before 329 that the baptism of Christians by birth was delayed till they were grown up),[3] we shall have to think of the children primarily as *their* children. 'Thus what we see happening is in fact the accession of "households" to the Christian fellowship' (J 75). Aland attempts to evade this interpretation of the text, which in my opinion is the most natural one, by pointing to the fact that the children are the first to be baptized and that for the smallest amongst them, who cannot yet speak (i.e. cannot answer the baptismal questions nor make the baptismal confession), 'their parents, or another who belongs to their family, should speak' (*Apostolic Tradition* 21.4). Aland comments on this rule: 'Only a full Christian is in a position to answer for others at baptism, as obtains even in baptismal prescriptions of today' (A 52) and draws far-reaching conclusions from this assertion. Since the catechumens at the moment of the children's baptism were not yet themselves baptized, and therefore—according to Aland—were by no means allowed to make the baptismal confession for their children, 'the infants and children' can only mean 'children of *Christian*

---

[1] *De baptismo* 19.1. I have not 'postulated' anywhere that Easter was the only day for baptizing catechumens, as Aland imputes to me (A 45). On the contrary I quoted from the Decretal of Pope Siricius that according to an old Roman custom it was permissible to baptize adults not only at Easter, but also in the season of rejoicing until Pentecost (J 74, n. 1). But it is well established that 'the general festival of baptism in the Church was from early days associated with the festival of the resurrection' (H. Usener, *Das Weihnachtsfest*[2], Bonn, 1911, 180f., references on 181f.).

[2] *Apostolic Tradition* 21.4f. Aland considers the possibility that the passage about the children might have been interpolated (A 49f.). The agreement shown by the Coptic, Ethiopic, Arabic and Syriac traditions just in this passage (J 3f.; 75, n. 1) certainly does not favour this hypothesis.

[3] J 88f.

families'. There is 'no alternative therefore but to interpret the infants as belonging to Christian parents' (A 52). Aland knows, too, what happened to the children, at any rate to the very smallest, of the newly baptized catechumens: they are 'evidently kept over to the next baptism, or to a later one' (A 52). The only ground on which this interpretation of *Apostolic Tradition* 21.4f. rests is 'the baptismal prescriptions of today'! Everything else is pure hypothesis. It is already exceedingly daring to bring in modern church regulations in order to explain a document of the years 215–220; still more disquieting is the fact that the argument does not even apply. What is the position? Is it really true that 'in baptismal prescriptions of today' 'only a full Christian' (i.e. one who has been baptized) is allowed to make the baptismal confession for his child? This confession has from the earliest days (the oldest evidence is in Acts 8.37) been made *before* baptism. Accordingly at the baptism of a family the parents even today make their baptismal confession before their actual baptism, that is, without being full Christians. What order of baptism would forbid them to answer the baptismal questions and to make the baptismal confession for their infant as well, when they are going to be baptized themselves immediately afterwards? What other course would, indeed could, a minister take today? I do not by any means maintain that the Easter season was 'exclusively' reserved for the baptism of catechumens, as Aland imputes to me (A 45f.), and that consequently the infants baptized at Easter must one and all have been the children of catechumens. On the contrary it seems to me very probable that Christian parents, too, had their latest-born children baptized at the solemn Easter baptism. However, the text gives no sort of pretext for the elimination of the children and infants of catechumens.

But if we are to see in the three divisions, children, men and women, in the main the families of catechumens, then it is natural to assume a continuous connexion with the baptism of the 'houses' reported in the Acts. Aland tries to call in question the continuity between the baptism of the houses described in the New Testament and the account of the baptism given by Hippolytus by considering the meaning and nature of Church Orders. It is usual for a Church Order to look to the future (A 51). 'Whatever belongs to the old order and is useful for the new is permitted to remain, but the really important thing to the composer of a Church Order is always the new, otherwise he would not have needed to write it.' Aland would like to include amongst these new things the baptism of infants as being, in his opinion, 'relatively new' as 'a general Church custom' (A 51). Does Hippolytus' *Apostolic Tradition* wish to preserve what is old or to introduce something new? His intention quite certainly is the former, as the title ἀποστολικὴ παράδοσις indeed indicates (it was hardly as clear to him as it is to us that he was, in fact, not using the adjective 'apostolic' in the historical sense, but as a theological value judgement). No doubt his Church Order reflects the time-honoured usages of his period in which earlier and later traditions were intermingled. But that makes no difference to his intention, expressly stated in the prologue, that to guard against heretical innovations he was codifying what had long been handed down.[1] The very paragraph about the baptism of 'houses' including the children is an example in point. It introduces no innovation which only through it acquired 'a regulation and anchorage in the baptismal ritual' (A 51). For the provision of proxies for the smallest children who cannot yet speak, which Hippolytus' *Apostolic Tradition* attests for Rome in 215, was already at the beginning of the century a regular custom in North Africa, as we learn from Tertullian.[2] Besides, there is no lack of evidence for the baptism of 'houses' during the interval between the New Testament and Hippolytus. For the first half of the second century we may name Aristides, who will be discussed in detail shortly, for the second half of the same century Tertullian, *De baptismo* 18.3–19.1[3, 4]

[1] E. Hauler, *Didascaliae Apostolorum fragmenta Ueronensia Latina* I, Leipzig, 1900, 101f.: *Nunc autem ex caritate, qua(m) in omnes sanctos habuit, producti ad uerticem traditionis, quae catecizat, ad ecclesias perreximus, ut [h]ii, qui bene ducti sunt, eam, quae permansit usq(ue) nunc, traditionem exponentibus nobis custodiant et agnoscentes firmiores maneant, propter eum, qui nuper inuentus est per ignorantiam lapsus uel error, et hos, qui ignorant, praestante s(an)c(t)o sp(irit)u perfectam gratiam eis, qui recte credunt, ut cognoscant, quomodo oportet tradi et custodiri omnia eos, qui ecclesiae praesunt.*

[2] *De Baptismo* 18.4 (between 200 and 206).

[3] The *sponsores* who make *promissiones* for the *parvuli* at the baptismal ceremony are most probably identical with the witnesses to character mentioned in the Church Orders who stood surety for those wishing to become converts when they applied for admission as catechumens. Their participation in baptism as godparents enables us to realize that in North Africa, too, 'houses' were baptized (cf. J 41).

[4] According to the *Chronicle of Arbela* (east of the Tigris in the Parthian empire) Bishop Noah (AD 151–67), who had himself been baptized as a small boy (ch. 13, F. Zorell, 'Chronica Ecclesiae Arbelensis', *Orientalia Christiana* 8, 1926/7, 157), baptized the village prefect 'Razšâḥ and the members of his household' (ch. 16, *op. cit.*, 159). But we disregard this statement, because the information in the Chronicle (composed before 569) is open to doubt in so far as it applies to earlier times (I. Ortiz de Urbina, 'Intorno al valore storico della Cronaca di Arbela', *Orientalia Christiana Periodica* 2, 1936, 5–32).

We do not learn so very much from Hippolytus about the practice of baptism of the 'houses'; nevertheless we do learn something. We are told that it took place in three parts (children, men, women) and that the parents said the baptismal confession for the smallest children. The separation of the sexes was certainly observed from the beginning at the baptism of the 'houses', since it was, of course, baptism by immersion and took place in the nude. We have already seen that the separate baptism of men and women is attested for proselyte baptism also.[1]

We shall still have to show that the result of our argument, namely that all the children were included in the baptism of the households on their conversion, agrees with the early Christian eschatological understanding of baptism.[2] We will conclude here by recalling I Cor. 10.1f., where Paul sketches the splendid picture of a collective baptism of the ancient people of God. By a great act of God, 'our fathers', when passing through the Red Sea 'were all together baptized' into Moses, a 'type' of the baptism of the new people of God. 'Our fathers all together' comprises the people of God in its completeness, men, women, children.[3]

---

[1] See above, p. 16. [2] See below, pp. 82ff.

[3] The Jewish traditions about the passage through the Red Sea concern themselves particularly with the children. References in Str. Bill. III, 406. I have attempted to show in 'Der Ursprung der Johannestaufe', *ZNW* 28, 1929, 312–20, that Paul was acquainted with old traditions of the Midrash concerning the story of the Red Sea passage.

III

An Age-limit
in the First Two Centuries?

WHEN DISCUSSING the Roman Easter baptism, as Hippolytus
(215–20) describes it for us, we reached the conclusion that at this
ceremony the 'houses' of the catechumens were admitted into the
congregation,[1] and the Pseudo-Clementine literature showed that
families as a whole were baptized amongst Jewish Christians as well.
It was natural to conjecture that a continuous connexion existed
with the baptism of the 'houses' in the apostolic and post-apostolic
period described in the New Testament. Such a connexion would, of
course, be impossible from the outset if it could be proved that
during the second century no longer whole 'houses', but only adults
had been baptized.

In fact this is what Aland maintains. He writes that 'prior to
this' (i.e. to the third century) 'we read only of the baptism of adults;
infant baptism appears to be excluded' (A 70). In order to do justice
to Aland we must indeed add immediately that he has framed his
sentence without due care. For the statement that up to AD 200 adults
only had been baptized does not in actual fact express his opinion.
For he says himself, four pages farther on, that we have 'an indubitable example of the baptism of children of maturer years' from the
end of the first century (A 74). Accordingly on pp. 101f. he introduces
qualifications; he now writes that the sources of the period before
AD 200 'have in view only the baptism of adults, or at best the baptism
of older children' (A 102). And even this wording is not careful
enough. To begin with, what is 'at best' intended to mean when 'the
baptism of children of maturer years' is admittedly confirmed by 'an
indubitable example' (A 74)? Surely 'at best' indicates the admission

---

[1] See above, pp. 28ff.

that the existence of a doubt is possible, but no one can challenge an 'indubitable example'. Is this not a case in which words are used—I quote—'in so unprecise a fashion that with the more[1] precise reader they produce favourable associations' (A 73)? But quite apart from this 'at best', is it really only 'children of maturer years' whose baptism Aland finds attested in the second century? We read on pp. 57f. that according to Aristides, *Apol.* 15.6, 'in the first decades of the second century' the children of Christian parents were baptized 'not before they have become several years old' (and so also on p. 72, n. 5)! But that is surely something other than 'children of maturer years'! To speak quite plainly, Aland, who is too sweeping in his summing up, has to admit in his detailed exposition that the Church practised child baptism all through the second century. I should like to underline this emphatically. Even according to Aland there can be no question of baptizing only adults in the second century. Aland merely asserts, like Windisch before him,[2] that an age-limit had existed. For he is of the opinion that in any case up to the end of the second century infants were excluded from baptism, and beyond this at least children until they 'have become several years old' (A 57). But whilst Windisch wished to fix the age-limit at the completion of the seventh year on the basis of psychological considerations ('At this age there was a knowledge of good and evil, feelings of guilt and a certain sense of responsibility, and a receptiveness for education and teaching',[3] Aland is inclined to name a later age after which children were baptized, namely puberty, i.e. about the age of fourteen (A 106, 111, cf. 66f.). Here he starts from a remark of Tertullian, not, in fact, referring to baptism, according to which the faculty of distinguishing good and evil appears as sexuality awakens. For this Tertullian appeals to the story of the fall (Gen. 3.7).[4] According to him the innocence of childhood ceases at puberty; only then does sinning come into existence (A 67); before that a cleansing bath for the forgiveness of sins is therefore superfluous (A 103f., 106). According to Aland considerations such as these guided the Church from its earliest days and induced it from the beginning not to baptize children until the 'age that required cleansing through the awakening of sin and the destruction of original purity' (A 107)—'Tertullian puts it at

---

[1] 'More' seems to be a slip of the pen for 'less.'
[2] 'Zum Problem der Kindertaufe im Urchristentum', *ZNW* 28, 1929, 132f.
[3] *Op. cit.*, 133. [4] *De anima* 38.1f.

the age of puberty' (A 111). This is not the place to discuss whether it is not a questionable proceeding to project backwards without more ado on to the primitive Church Tertullian's views, which are to a large extent stamped with his self-willed and independent-minded anthropology; it will have to be discussed later on, and in particular whether the restriction of baptismal grace to the remission of sins in *De baptismo* 18.5 (*quid festinat innocens aetas ad remissionem peccatorum?*) can be attributed so simply to the apostolic period.[1] Here we are merely concerned to show by what path Aland arrived at his opinion that the primitive Church had already observed an age-limit for baptism. In this matter he is careful enough not to commit himself to fourteen years of age; children were baptized when they had attained the faculty of self-knowledge (A 107), when they had 'reached a certain age' (A 111); but yet he is inclined to think that with Tertullian we must regard this 'certain age' as being simply puberty. Not until the rise of the doctrine of original sin (not yet in its developed form, but in its initial stages) towards the end of the second century does he think that all postponement of baptism was abandoned for children.

Now the conclusion which we have reached so far in chapter I, namely that already in apostolic times the complete family was baptized at the baptism of the 'houses', certainly does not favour the assumption of an age limit at the outset. So we inquire expectantly what sources Aland cites to substantiate his theory that an age-limit was observed at baptism from the very beginning. Here to be sure a great disappointment awaits us. For there is nowhere to be found any direct evidence for the thesis that the great Church[2] of the first two centuries had excluded from baptism any age group, e.g. infants, let alone any information about an age-limit. On the contrary Aland has to rely on inferences from I Cor. 7.14c, from the baptismal rite (including the preparation for baptism) and from the fourth-century practice of postponing baptism. In addition he appeals to two passages which according to his opinion point to an age-limit, namely to Aristides, *Apol.* 15.6, and an inscription (admittedly originating only in the third century). Let us follow these up.

---

[1] See below, pp. 82ff.
[2] We must disregard here the Marcionite church, which admitted to baptism only those who made a vow of celibacy or of continence in marriage (cf. J 69f.).

1. INFERENCES

(a) *Inferences from I Cor.* 7.14c

In the earliest days of Christianity—according to Aland—'infant baptism was not practised . . . since these infants were regarded as ἄγια' (A 113). Aland is therefore of the opinion that already Paul dispensed with the baptism of infants, or at least postponed it, and that I Cor. 7.14c enables us to see the reason for this: 'Your children . . . are holy' (τὰ τέκνα ὑμῶν . . . ἄγιά ἐστιν). It is true that Aland would not use the expressions 'dispensing with baptism' or 'postponement of baptism'. The terms such as 'forbearing to baptize', 'postponement of baptism', 'missionary baptism' originate, he says, in 'categories of thought' which 'do not do justice to the actual situation of the early Church' (A 108). 'Jeremias' argumentation is determined by modern ideas' (A 109). To these quite extraordinary assertions I can only ask in reply: Does Aland know nothing about the Jewish circumcision of infants and proselyte baptism? Does he wish to deny that this is the world out of which Paul comes? In his arguments Aland refers twice to 'modern ideas': 'even in baptismal prescriptions of today' 'only a full Christian' may render the baptismal confession on behalf of his children (A 52); 'even churches of our day refuse to baptize children of parents who do not belong to the Church' (A 77, n. 3), and therefore in both passages he reaches highly disputable conclusions. In no single passage in my book do I appeal to modern analogies, but adhere strictly to the historical data. When I speak about 'missionary baptism' and 'dispensing with baptism', my criteria are taken, not as Aland imputes to me, from modern baptismal practice, but from that of Judaism. It is there that the proselytes received a 'missionary baptism' and that baptism was 'dispensed with' in the case of proselytes' infants, if born after their mother's baptism. Conceptions alien to the period of primitive Christianity come into play only if it is assumed, as it is by Aland, that the baptism of children is postponed; for Judaism knows of no such thing. Not until the Church of the fourth century is there any evidence for it, and this is one of the reasons why the theory that it was the practice in the first century to postpone baptism is suspect from the start.

Let us leave terminology and return to the subject itself. Aland's inference that in primitive Christianity 'infant baptism was not practised . . . since these infants were regarded as ἅγια' (A 113), completely overlooks the fact that after all not all infants were considered to be 'holy', but *only* Christian ones (including the children of mixed marriages). Children of Gentiles, and therefore also infants of households contemplating conversion, were 'unclean', like their parents. If therefore it is thought that we may draw any inferences at all from I Cor. 7.14c, we must conclude that Paul did not baptize infants born in Christian marriage, because they were considered to be holy, and that on the other hand it was his practice to baptize children of converted houses because they were considered unclean. But that would be a conclusion which would upset Aland's whole conception. For the very thing he wants to demonstrate is that infant baptism was not practised at all before the end of the second century. Consequently in Aland's place I should prefer to give up altogether any inferences from I Cor. 7.14c and I would confine myself to a *non liquet*, which might be substantiated by pointing out that after all the text does not, in fact, mention baptism.

For my part, I do not think that we are justified in resigning ourselves so hastily. In the exegesis of I Cor. 7.14c we must start with the statement that the terms 'unclean' and 'holy' (ἀκάθαρτα/ἅγια) are derived from the language of Jewish ritual.[1] Aland indeed (A 81, 105) considers it possible, together with W. G. Kümmel,[2] that we are concerned here with 'popular notions'. But the explanation breaks down because there is no evidence at all outside Jewish literature for the pair of opposites ἀκάθαρτα/ἅγια. Now the Judaism of antiquity did baptize children 'not born in holiness' (i.e. before the mother's conversion to Judaism);[3] therefore in view of the extensive contacts between primitive Christian baptismal practice and the practice of proselyte baptism (see pp. 27f.) it is highly probable that the use of Jewish ritual terms in I Cor. 7.14c points to a similar Christian practice, namely that at the conversion of the 'houses' all the children were baptized, too.

On the other hand, I Cor. 7.14c does not enable a reliable inference to be drawn regarding the question whether or not the children of Christian parents were baptized in Corinth. In antiquity Judaism did not baptize children 'born in holiness' (i.e. *after* the

---

[1] LXX Lev. 10.10; 11.43f.; 12.4; 20.25f.; Judg. 13.7 B; Job 15.15f.; Isa. 35.8; 52.1; Ezek. 22.26; 44.23.
[2] H. Lietzmann–W. G. Kümmel, *An die Korinther I, II*[4], Tübingen, 1949, 177.
[3] *b. Yebamot* 78a. Cf. J 46.

conversion of their mother).[1] It might be assumed at first sight that a similar practice was followed in the Christian church in Corinth. I had reasoned in this way on pp. 52–56 of my book in the original German edition, and concluded that Christian parents in Corinth dispensed with the baptism of their children. But I soon let myself be convinced (J 47f.) that this conclusion overlooked the fact that in Judaism, on the mother's conversion, although the children thus born 'in holiness' were not baptized, yet the boys were circumcised. Now amongst the Pauline congregations baptismal immersion took over the function of circumcision as the seal of membership in God's people; so there is just as much reason, indeed perhaps more reason, for the conclusion that, as Judaism circumcised male infants even when born 'in holiness', so Christians baptized children even when born as 'holy' (ἅγια). After all, the 'sanctification' of the pagan husband or wife did not in any way exclude his or her conversion and baptism.[2]

It is clear that inferences concerning baptismal practice with regard to Christian children based on I Cor. 7.14c are unreliable. We must be content to state—and the same applies to Acts 21.21—that our curiosity remains unsatisfied. Only one thing must be considered certain, namely that the term 'unclean' (ἀκάθαρτα) makes it highly probable that the children of pagan descent were baptized together with their parents on their conversion.

(b) Inferences from the baptismal rite?

Next it is information of the second century concerning the baptismal rite from which Aland thinks that he can gather indications of an age-limit observed for baptism (A 53f.). In AD 150 baptism seems to have been preceded by a period of probation (cf. Hermas, *Vis.* III, 7.3); before that by instruction for baptism, which, according to *Did.* 1–6, contains warnings against dreadful sins such as are not yet within a child's range; before baptism the candidate is to fast for one or two days (7.4); the Eucharist follows baptism (Justin, *Apol.* I, 65.5); all these practices 'make the presupposition of a participation of infants in the baptismal event

---

[1] *b. Yebamot* 78a.
[2] Cf. W. Metzger, 'Wird in I Kor. 7.14c ein Taufverzicht sichtbar?', *Deutsches Pfarrerblatt* 59, 1959, 269–71; Chr. Maurer, review in *Kirchenblatt für die reformierte Schweiz* 115, 1959, 140; cf. also A. Richardson, *An Introduction to the Theology of the New Testament*, London, 1958, 359.

appear unthinkable' (A 55). Besides, the subject-matter of the instruction, judging by what can be gathered from *Did*. 1–6, excludes in addition 'both children and those who are growing up' (A 53f.).

However, it is not so certain as Aland makes out that all these rites were out of the question in the case of infants and little children. For instance, there is evidence amongst the Jews of partial fasting by small children on the Day of Atonement (*Soph*. 18.5; cf. J 49); as concerns the Eucharist, Aland himself (A 57) thinks it possible (in my opinion hardly correctly) that the communion of small children attested by Cyprian for the third century[1] was already customary at the beginning of the second century. Nevertheless, let us disregard such details and at once put the fundamental question: is it permissible to extract from statements about the baptismal procedure actual inferences concerning an age limit (exclusion of infants, children and adolescents)? In the tractate *Gerim* the regulations for admission to proselyte baptism and for its procedure are collected; they are framed entirely to suit adults. Are children therefore excluded? By no means! In 3.8, dealing with the legal position of proselytes regarding their right of inheritance, children appear surprisingly in a subordinate clause: 'when a proselyte dies and leaves a son, or a daughter, who has become a proselyte with him . . .' Analogous observations can be made in the rabbinic regulations concerning the passover meal and the feast of Tabernacles. The ritual of the passover meal does provide for the participation of children, yet only of such as can ask questions and receive instruction (*Pes*. 10.4). Only from a chance remark do we learn that tiny children, too, were present at table: a piece of passover *mazza* was put into their mouth so that they should not go to sleep during the service (*Tos. Pes*. 10.9 p. 172.27–173.1). As concerns the feast of Tabernacles, according to *Sukka* 2.8 women, slaves and minors were not obliged to live in the booth; an addendum extends the obligation to those boys under age who no longer needed their mothers. But we only learn from a particular incident that specially zealous people applied the regulation to infants, too. Shammai the Elder (*c*. 20 BC) broke up the roof above his daughter-in-law's bed and covered the opening with branches so that his newborn grandson might comply with the regulation (*loc. cit.*). Amongst the

---

[1] *De lapsis* 9, 25; cf. J 85.

primitive Christians the situation was no different. If we read Tertullian's statement about baptismal confession made 'with our mouth' (*ore nostro*, *De spectaculis* 4.1), about abrenunciation (*De corona* 3.2), about the newly baptized persons giving up their daily bath for a week after baptism (3.3), we should certainly at first be inclined to agree with Aland's conclusion that all this 'surely does not have infants in view' (A 64); Tertullian, in fact, clearly has in view 'the baptism of adults or of those who had recently come to mature years' (A 63). And yet we learn from *De baptismo* 18.4f. that *infantes*, too, were baptized and that the difficulty was met by *sponsores* making the baptismal confession as their proxies.[1] The position in the *Apostolic Tradition* of Hippolytus is just the same. Everything that is said about admission to the catechumenate (16), the catechumens' probationary period of three years (17), their participation in the church service (18f.), the baptism of blood (19.2), the preparations immediately preceding baptism (20), all this applies only to adults. Quite unexpectedly children and infants appear in the rules about the procedure at the baptism (21.4). Thus Jewish and Christian baptismal orders alike start with adults as the normal case without on that account excluding children. It is, moreover, quite easy to understand why the order was framed to suit adults. On the one hand, less attention was paid to the children; they were, so to speak, hidden in the bosom of their family; on the other hand, there is the additional fact, in the baptismal order especially, that the rite had of necessity to be simplified for small children and any part to be played by the candidate had to be completely omitted in the case of infants. It is therefore an exceedingly questionable proceeding to draw inferences about an age-limit from the statements concerning baptismal rites. The same applies also to inferences from baptismal instruction. When, for instance, in *Did.* 2.2, in the teaching of the 'Two Ways' (1-6), we read: 'Mix no poison, do not procure the abortion of a child in the womb, nor kill it when it is born', this can most certainly be said only to adults. Yet it is not permissible to draw the conclusion that the way in which the baptismal instruction is framed (on the assumption that the doctrine of the Two Ways in the *Didache* is intended for this purpose) demonstrates that in AD 100 not only infants and little children, but also older 'children and those who are growing up' (A 53f.) were excluded from baptism.

[1] See below p. 65.

For this inference overlooks the fact that it is simply traditional for baptismal orders to have the baptism of adults in view without on that account leaving out the children.

It seems to me that there is far greater justification for putting forward the opposite argument, considering the correspondence down to details between proselyte baptism and primitive Christian baptism (in terminology, instruction, external rite and the illustrative material used to interpret it).[1] The argument would then run: if the Jewish baptismal order includes children, although it does not expressly mention them, this will be equally true of the Christian references to the baptismal rite. They will in the same way tacitly comprise children even if they are framed for adults. This much at least must be said: the early Christian descriptions of the rite afford no warrant for the hypothesis of an age-limit.

(c) Inferences from the postponement of baptism?

Lastly we must mention a third inference used by Aland to support an age limit. He appeals to the custom found in the fourth century of postponing baptism, if possible, until the hour of death. This custom according to Aland's argument 'could certainly not have originated *ex nihilo*' (A 100f.). 'It is not something new and unheard of, as Jeremias would have us believe' (A 101). On the contrary 'it can be satisfactorily explained only when it is recognized' that beside infant baptism there 'existed a baptism of children of a mature age' (A 101). 'The only new thing about it is the scrupulousness observed in the Emperor Constantine and others, who waited for baptism until such time as it seemed to them to guarantee their salvation with certainty' (A 101). This 'postponement of baptism' would then 'in reality' represent 'the last epoch of the practice of the ancient Church' (A 101). This means that the new thing was not the postponement of baptism itself, but the extension of the age-limit, which according to Aland had been observed in the first centuries and was placed at about fourteen years, even perhaps a little earlier. Baptism was now postponed not only until the age of reason, but further on, if possible to the approach of death. Now, this inference associates two phenomena of a completely different nature. For the postulated baptism of 'children of mature years' (assuming that it existed as a custom of the Church) would have been a usage practised

---

[1] J 29-37.

within the congregation for children of Christian parents or of parents converted to the Christian faith. On the other hand the postponement of baptism until the hour of death (or until a critical illness) came into use in circles sympathizing with the Church and yet standing outside it. This is shown at once by the earliest example of it, the 'clinical' baptism[1] of Novatian (middle of the third century), of whom it is stated explicitly that he had not belonged to the Church originally.[2] It is certainly not fortuitous that the custom of postponing baptism until shortly before death became prevalent when Christianity was recognized by the State and when, in consequence, people crowded into the Church. These large numbers often brought with them a purely superstitious understanding of baptism. Because many of the pagans turning to the Church saw in baptism exclusively the sacrament for a complete remission of sins, they postponed it until their deathbed, if possible; for they believed that by securing baptismal purity they would be sure of eternal life. It was considered to be the greatest good fortune to die 'in the white [sc. baptismal robe]' (*in albis*), as inscriptions ('died in the white', *in albis decessit*) confirm. It was only secondarily that this example was followed by the community as well and that it induced Christian parents, too, to postpone the baptism of their children.[3] The earliest evidence that Christian parents did not have a child baptized immediately after birth comes from the year 329-30. It concerns Gregory of Nazianzus, who although the son of a bishop was not baptized as a child, but did not let himself be baptized until *c.* 360, after a storm on the journey from Alexandria to Athens had forcibly conjured up the dangers of sudden death (J 88).[4] The fact that such a postponement of baptism in the case of children of Christian parents was not yet practised in the third century is confirmed *e silentio* by the *Acts of the Martyrs*, at any rate so far as can be learned from the collection of

[1] Baptism on his bed by affusion.
[2] Eusebius, *Hist. Eccl.* VI, 43.13–15.
[3] I collected the material on pp. 87f. of my book. I request readers of it to cross out the two words 'and baptism' on p. 87, ll. 4 and 5. Aland is correct in remarking (A 67f.) that Tertullian in *De paenitentia* 6.3–24 is not objecting to postponement of baptism, but to the opinion of catechumens that until baptism they need not take Christian ethics as seriously as full Christians.
[4] The next instance is Basil the Great, born in 330-1 as the child of Christian parents and baptized in 358 (J 88). As regards Basil, a passing comment may be made on Aland's remark (p. 101); we have no evidence, so far as I know, that he called 'for the early baptism of children with complete lack of prejudice'. The correct state of affairs is given in J (p. 89).

R. Knopf and G. Krüger, and from Eusebius' work on the Palestinian martyrs in the years 303–11.[1]

The custom of postponing baptism until the hour of death (or until ordination as a priest)[2] has therefore not developed out of an earlier custom of conferring baptism at the age of puberty (there is no support whatever for this hypothesis). It was a practice which arose in the third century amongst pagans ready for conversion, became prevalent in the fourth century in consequence of the change of the political position of the Church in the era of Constantine, and was met half-way by increasing scrupulosity on the part of the congregations who shied away from the heavy obligations which awaited the full Christian.

*   *   *

Apart from the inferences we have discussed, Aland can quote from the writings of the second century—that is to say from the period before direct evidence of the practice of infant baptism is available—only one single passage to support his theory of an age-limit: the *Apology* of Aristides 15.6. It is to this that we must now turn.

2. ARISTIDES, *Apology* 15.6

The passage is preserved in Greek on Pap. Br. Mus. 2486, and, in addition, in the Syriac translation which we render as literally as possible (the Armenian version is lacking).

Papyrus 2486 recto, lines 7–11	*Syriac translation*
ἀλλὰ καὶ δούλους	but slaves
ἢ παιδίσκας	and maidservants
ἐὰν ἔχωσιν	or children
ἢ τέκνα	if some of them have (any)
πείθουσιν αὐτοὺς	they persuade them
χρειστιανοὺς γενέσθαι	to become Christians

[1] R. Knopf and G. Krüger, *Ausgewählte Märtyrerakten* (Sammlung ausgewählter kirchen- und dogmengeschichtlicher Quellenschriften, N.F. 3)³, Tübingen, 1929; A. Bigelmair, *Des Eusebius Pamphili Schrift über die Märtyrer in Palästina* (Bibliothek der Kirchenväter 9)², Kempten–München, 1913. If the baptism of Christian children had already in the period before Constantine been postponed until adulthood, as became customary in the fourth century, then the *Acts of the Martyrs* would sometimes have mentioned that unbaptized Christians were baptized before their death, or that their death was considered to be a baptism of blood, especially as a regular point is made, wherever possible, of emphasizing that the martyrs had been Christians continuously since childhood.

[2] It is well known that Ambrose was elected Bishop of Milan in 374 whilst unbaptized and was consecrated as bishop eight days after his baptism.

ἵνα ἔχωσιν εὐνόους	because of their love of them
καὶ ὅταν γένωνται τοιοῦτοι	and when they have become such
ἀδελφοὺς καλοῦσι αὐτοὺς	they call them brothers
ἀμέριστοι ὄντες[1]	without (making) a distinction[2]

We must first examine the question whether the *Apology* of Aristides really belongs in the period before AD 200 with which we are concerned. Until recently there was general agreement that it should be attributed to the second century AD. The only matter in dispute was whether it ought to be assigned with Eusebius[3] and with the title of the Armenian translation to the reign of Hadrian (117–38), or whether, on the evidence of the Syriac translation which lets the *Apology* be addressed to Antoninus Pius as well as to Hadrian, it should be ascribed to the reign of Antoninus Pius (138–61). But in 1958 G. C. O'Ceallaigh vigorously challenged this *consensus doctorum*.[4] He propounds the opinion that the original version of the *Apology* was a Jewish work from the time of Hadrian, and that much later, between 360 and 400, a Christian made interpolations in it and published it anew. Amongst his arguments for ascribing Aristides' *Apology* in its present form to the late fourth century a prominent place is occupied by his appeal to the Christological formula 'having descended from heaven . . . and from the (holy) virgin . . . he put on flesh' (ἀπ᾽ οὐρανοῦ καταβὰς . . . καὶ ἐκ παρθένου (ἁγίας) . . . σάρκα ἀνέλαβε), which O'Ceallaigh extracts from 2.6. He says that this formula only came into general use in Syria in the late fourth century, as he concludes from *Const. Apost.* VII, 41.6,[5] and that therefore the *Apology* must have acquired its Christian form in this period. But things are not at all so simple. The end of the fourth century is in itself too late for an Apology; moreover, this date for the work can be definitely ruled out by a fact completely overlooked by O'Ceallaigh, namely that Pap. Br. Mus. 2486, containing a part of the *Apology* which can have come only from a Christian (15.5–16.1), must, for palaeographic reasons, be

---

[1] H. J. M. Milne, 'A New Fragment of the Apology of Aristides', *Journal of Theological Studies* 25, 1923/4, 73–77, here p. 74.

[2] J. R. Harris, *The Apology of Aristides* (Texts and Studies I, 1), Cambridge, 1891, p. 24, ll. 5–8 of the Syriac text.

[3] *Hist. Eccl.* IV, 3.3.

[4] '"Marcianus" Aristides, On the Worship of God', *Harvard Theological Review* 51, 1958, 227–54.

[5] F. X. Funk, *Didascalia et Constitutiones Apostolorum* I, Paderborn, 1905, 446.7 (Greek), 447.6 (Syr.).

assigned to the early fourth century.[1] As regards the Christological formula (and the formulae of its context!) the question of its age needs a more thorough investigation than can be given here. I hope that this brief critical report has at least made it evident that the question of dating the *Apology* has recently come *sub judice*. However, my personal opinion is that the impression of antiquity made by the sections on the Christian religion justifies the continued ascription of the *Apology* in its present form to the second century. Thus the question of its date would not make me hesitate to use the *Apology*, although an uncertainty about it remains.

Next I must say a word about the relationship between the two forms of the text printed side by side on pp. 43f. above. Pap. 2486 contains *Apol.* 15.5 (end) to 16.1 in Greek. A detailed comparison with the completely preserved Syriac translation shows that this has caught the meaning in general, but that it tends to amplify, translates inaccurately at times, omits what it does not understand, and above all has not fully preserved the naive, awkward, style of the Greek text. All in all the Greek text is unquestionably the more original one.

The point at issue in the text is a single word, namely the word 'children' (τέκνα, *bny*'). According to Aland, this passage speaks 'unequivocally of the children of Christians'. The Syriac text 'cannot be so translated as if it referred to children of the maidservants and servants'. But the Greek text, too, 'makes it impossible to understand the τέκνα as children of the servants.' . . . 'A baptism of these children while still infants is excluded.' On the contrary, 'the impression is given that they are baptized only after they have attained the needful insight, hence not before they have become several years old. Then they are baptized and, despite their youth, are regarded as full Christians, and they participate in the eucharist (a custom which is also attested by Cyprian in the third century)' (A 57). Here, then, we might have some support for an age-limit for the baptism of Christian children, even if it is somewhat indefinite. Baptism does not take place until they are old enough to be 'instructed' (*loc. cit.*). However, that is not in the text. *Mpysyn lhwn* does not say 'they instruct them', but like the πείθουσιν αὐτούς of the Greek, that 'they persuade them', which hardly suits the small children of Christian parents.

Thus at this point at the latest we are led to the question: is it really so 'unequivocal' as Aland maintains (*loc. cit.*) that our text

[1] Milne, *op. cit.*, 73.

concerns children of Christian parents? In fact, this interpretation of τέκνα encounters great difficulties.

Let us begin with the final sentence: 'when they have become Christians they call them brothers without making a distinction.' According to Aland this sentence states that 'despite their youth' (*loc. cit.*) the children are distinguished after their baptism by the name of brother. This explanation seems to me not to do justice to the text. Whatever the interpretation given to τέκνα, the final sentence can refer only to slaves and maidservants. After all, the author wants to praise the exemplary social behaviour of Christians; he mentions as a particularly impressive example their custom of calling the slaves and maidservants brothers, when they become Christians, ἀμέριστοι ὄντες ('because they [as a community] are [an] indivisible [unity]'). All social discrimination ceases to exist in the Church. The correctness of this interpretation of the last sentence is confirmed by the fact that the phrase *dl' pwlg* ('without making a distinction') with which the Syriac renders the end of our quotation appears again in the Syriac translation of Acts 11.12 (μηδὲν διακρί-ναντα); there it denotes the end of religious discrimination against pagans. So then, the conferring of the name 'brother' certainly does not have in view the children of the Christian householders. Indeed, secondly, we must go further. Everything which follows the word τέκνα refers to the servants: πείθουσιν αὐτοὺς χρειστιανοὺς γενέσθαι (does not fit their own dependent children), ἵνα ἔχωσιν εὐνόους (εὔνους, 'devoted, willing' is a virtue typical of slaves), καὶ ὅταν γένωνται τοιοῦτοι ἀδελφοὺς καλοῦσιν αὐτούς (Philem. 16; I Tim. 6.2 of slaves), ἀμέριστοι ὄντες (all social discrimination disappears).[1]

---

[1] Aland renders this text as follows: 'The children of Christian families are "instructed, that they become Christians". This happens out of love for them, for they also should become partakers of the blessings of Christ's people. "And when they have become Christians [through baptism] they call them 'brethren' without distinction"' (A 107). On this we must comment: (*a*) As we have already said, 'instruct' occurs neither in the Greek nor in the Syriac text. (*b*) The first and third of Aland's three sentences are translations; the middle one ('this happens out of love for them, for they also should become partakers of the blessings of Christ's people'), on the other hand, gives us only a paraphrase, clearly because in this sentence Aland deserts the (more original!) Greek text (ἵνα ἔχωσιν εὐνόους) which only suits slaves, and follows the Syriac one which is ambiguous ('because of their love for them *dç'dyhwn*'). Aland makes this phrase apply to the love of the parents towards their children. But he overlooks the fact that the Syriac text here must be interpreted with the Greek in mind, i.e. it most probably means 'because of the love (which the slaves should have) to them' (cf. with this 15.10: 'God's favour *dç'dyhwn* to them', i.e. which God shows to them). This means that Aland's attempt to make the second part of our text (from πείθουσιν αὐτούς) indicate the children of Christian parents comes to grief—apart from everything else—over the ἵνα ἔχωσιν εὐνόους of the Greek text, which suits only slaves.

We come, thirdly, going backwards, to the beginning of the text in which the decisive word τέκνα occurs: 'but even slaves or maidservants, if they have (any), or children' (ἀλλὰ καὶ δούλους ἢ παιδίσκας ἐὰν ἔχωσιν ἢ τέκνα). Here it is noticeable that in the Syriac text the limiting phrase 'if some of them have (any)' does not occur until after the word 'children'. Aland understands by the 'children' the children of the Christian householders, and deduces from the Syriac text the statement that it was exceptional for Christian houses to have children. He says that 'the number of children born in Christian marriages . . . in the first decades of the second century is not particularly large', their existence is not assumed 'as the rule' (A 58). But there is nothing to justify the extremely unlikely assumption that in Aristides' time the great majority of Christian marriages were childless. On the contrary, the text of the Greek papyrus, the more original one, as already noted, shows that the limitation 'if they have (any)' (ἐὰν ἔχωσιν) refers to the slaves and maidservants. The presence of servants (not the presence of children!) was not taken for granted in Christian houses. But in that case the Syriac translator, who evidently brought forward 'or children' (ἢ τέκνα) simply to make the text run more smoothly, must have conceived the triad of slaves, maidservants and children to be a unit and thought of the children as sons and daughters of the slaves. That such is really the meaning of both texts is supported, fourthly, by the order in which the children are mentioned and by the casual way in which they are added on. For if Aristides had really been speaking of the children of the house, it would certainly be very strange for him to have referred to them only after the servants and mentioned them merely as an afterthought;[1] on the other hand, it is quite appropriate for the children of slaves to be specially mentioned because, as K. H. Rengstorf points out to me, matrimonial unions between slaves were not regarded as marriages in the proper sense of the word. It would be remarkable, too, that the following lines should have ignored the children of the householders completely (we have already seen that everything coming after τέκνα applies to the servants). Fifthly and lastly, we must refer to the context. The *Apology* introduces the subject by describing, with the help of examples taken partly from

---

[1] In the Greek text, which, as noted, is the more original, ἢ τέκνα is an addendum. Aland's conjecture that in it ἐὰν ἔχωσιν 'possibly (and rightly?) relates . . . only to the servants and maidservants' (A 57, n. 5) is erroneous. How does he construe the sentence if 'or children' (ἢ τέκνα) is not governed by 'if they have' (ἐὰν ἔχωσιν)?

the Decalogue, partly from the Sermon on the Mount, how Christians observe the commands of Jesus Christ (15.3–5). Next, attention is directed to actual areas of life. The exemplary quality of the Christians' family life with its sexual purity is emphasized (15.6a). Then follows their generous social behaviour, our passage (15.6b). To this is attached an account of the manifestation of love in the Church (15.7–9), etc. This train of thought also makes it very unlikely that family life, which had been dealt with in 6a, would be referred to again in 6b by way of the children. And even if, in spite of all this, the interpretation of the τέκνα as the children of Christian householders were upheld, the question would still have to be asked whether these τέκνα must still be children. For grown-up[1] sons and daughters with their own households might also be in mind and the converted parents might be urging them also to decide to become Christians. 'They persuade them to become Christians' (πείθουσιν αὐτοὺς χρειστιανοὺς γενέσθαι) is at any rate more suitable for adults than for small children. Yet this way out is hardly practicable either. On the contrary, as my colleague, Wolf-Hartmut Friedrich emphatically corroborates, there is every likelihood that the τέκνα mentioned as a kind of addendum means the children of the slaves and maidservants. But in that case our text provides evidence, not for an age-limit, but for the baptism of 'houses'. For we learn from Aristides, *Apol.* 15.6, that the slaves also, if they were married and had children, were admitted as families into the Church.[2]

* * *

For the sake of completeness it should be mentioned that Aland also adduces inferences from Clement of Alexandria and Tertullian in support of his theory of an age-limit for children. Clement (died

---

[1] Cf. I Tim. 5.4; Justin, *Dial.* 19.4; 138.1; *Apol.* II, 1.2.

[2] On pp. 70f. of my book I had introduced Aristides, *Apol.* 15.11, though rather cautiously, as indirect evidence for the baptism of the children of Christian parents; I did so, in fact, because of the phrase 'they thank God' (εὐχαριστοῦσιν τῷ θεῷ) which recurs in 17.4 in a context suggesting baptism. Aland contradicts this on pp. 55ff. because, as I myself had mentioned, the phrase occurs again in 15.10 to describe morning prayers and grace at meals, and twice in 15.11 for the ceremony at the death of a church member. Aland's objection is no doubt justified lexically. On the other hand, it must not be overlooked that, in all the passages, 'to give thanks' (εὐχαριστεῖν) evidently indicates not a spontaneous expression of gratitude, but a regular liturgical usage. Since we now know from 15.6 that according to Aristides in any case the children of pagan slaves when converted were baptized, we must continue to consider the question whether the 'thanksgiving' mentioned in 15.11 at the birth of a Christian child is not a short way of speaking of its baptism, especially since Aristides deliberately avoids direct mention of the sacraments.

before AD 215) often speaks of baptism. 'Out of the more than twenty passages listed by Stählin in his index (among which those relating to παῖς, νήπιος, etc., must be reckoned) the conclusion seems clear to me that the baptism of children falls outside the range of Clement's view (to choose a cautious mode of expression); i.e. either it is without significance for *him*, or it does not exist for his time' (A 59). The first alternative is correct. For when Clement, as Aland explains on p. 59, constantly interprets the New Testament passages mentioning children allegorically to mean adults, that does not, of course, prove that children did not exist then, but merely that they were 'without significance' for Clement.

So far as Tertullian is concerned, it is well known that he rejects the baptism of *infantes*. 'So let them come when they are bigger, when they (can) learn, when they (can) be taught where to come; let them become Christians when they are able to know Christ' (*ueniant ergo dum adolescunt, dum discunt, dum quo ueniant docentur; fiant Christiani cum Christum nosse potuerint*).[1] 'Obviously that corresponds not only to what he believes to be right but to the practice of the Church hitherto' (A 106). But there is just nothing of this in the text 'at least when allowed (its) literal sense' (A 102). Here 'unproven presuppositions are utilized and are taken as self-evident, although they are nothing of the sort' (A 42), as we shall see on pp. 64ff.

But Aland has still a final text to offer us which is intended to provide evidence for the age-limit for children, namely the Marcianus inscription.

3. THE MARCIANUS INSCRIPTION (AD 268)

Pasto[r et T]i[t]iana et <dove> Marciana et <leaf>
Chr[e]st[e Mar]ciano filio benemerenti [in]
Xρ. dn. fec[eru]n[t] qui uixit annus XII m(enses) II et d[ies . . .]
qui cra[tiam][2] accepit d.n. die XII ka[l.O]ctob[r]es [Ma]
5 *[rini]ano (et) Paterno II coss. et rede[dit][3] XI ka[l. ss. ?]*
uibas (= vivas) inter sanctis in a[eternum][4]

---

[1] *De baptismo* 18.5.
[2] I.e. baptism.   [3] Sc. *spiritum*.
[4] E. Diehl, *Lateinische altchristliche Inschriften* (Kleine Texte 26–28)[2], Bonn, 1913, 29, No. 164; E. Diehl. *Inscriptiones Latinae Christianae Veteres* II, Berlin, 1927, No. 3315; J 80; A 78. Rome, S. Callisto.

Pastor and Titiana and Marciana and
Chreste for Marcianus (their) worthy son in
Christ the Lord made (this inscription), who lived 12 years,
    2 months and . . . days
who received the grace of our Lord on the 12th day before the
    Kalends of October, Ma-
rinianus and Paternus II being consuls, and rendered (his soul)
    on the 11th day before the Ka[lends . . .
Live among the saints in eternity.

This inscription, so Aland declares, by its text (ll. 2f., 4, 6) as well as by its symbols 'shows itself unambiguously to be Christian'. 'Pagan parents' are 'absolutely' out of the question. 'This particular child of Christian parents in Rome was not baptized till he was over twelve years old! The inscription actually shatters the thesis that infant baptism was administered to Christian children, and at the same time it tears a very large hole in the idea that infant baptism was obligatory in the third century.' On the contrary this was 'not observed without exception'. Finally Aland brings his arguments to an end by declaring not without emphasis that this inscription 'shows conclusively how impossible the theory of Jeremias is, that all baptisms at a later age were of such as were converted from without, and that children of Christian parents were normally baptized as children or infants' (A 78f.).

I believe that fairness demands that I should start by correcting a misleading phrase used by Aland. Aland says that the Marcianus inscription 'shatters the thesis that infant baptism was administered to Christian children, and at the same time . . . the idea that infant baptism was obligatory in the third century' (A 78f.). I puzzled my brains for a long time about the first phrase. Aland cannot possibly mean that at the period of the inscription infant baptism was not administered to Christian children; in the words immediately following he really only doubts whether it had been obligatory in the third century. And after all this year, AD 268, is in a period for which the practice of infant baptism is attested beyond question by literary evidence (Tertullian, Hippolytus, Origen, Cyprian!). If I understand Aland aright, he has expressed himself too concisely and therefore misleadingly. He clearly wishes to say that the inscription shatters the thesis that *in the first two centuries it was already the practice* to baptize Christian children in infancy. So his argument runs as follows: not until the beginning of the third century is infant baptism reliably attested. Therefore it was an innovation. But if in AD 268 a Christian child, twelve years of age, is still unbaptized and receives baptism only when on his deathbed, it can be conjectured that an earlier custom is being carried on, namely that of baptizing only 'children of a mature age' (A 101). In that case we should have here at last and for the first time support for an age-limit for baptism which Aland maintains for the period before AD 180, even though this evidence would be decidedly late and indirect. For we should merely learn that in the year 268 a twelve-year-old 'child of Christian parents' was not yet baptized, but not to what age it was the custom to postpone the baptism of children.

But is the Marcianus inscription really the reliable evidence which is being sought for the postponement of baptism in the first Christian centuries? The answer is soon supplied. Aland himself (A 43f.) describes how the catechumens, especially after the three-year probationary period was introduced (Hippolytus, *Apostolic Tradition* 17.1), already virtually belonged to the Church before their baptism, even though they were excluded from the Eucharist and the kiss of peace. If a child belonging to such a catechumen died during the period of probation, how should the inscription on the tomb be worded in any but Christian terms? The possibility that the twelve-year-old Marcianus was the child of a catechumen is incontestable. The inscription on his tomb comes from Rome and belongs to the second half of the third century, thus to a period in which catechumens made up a considerable part of the community in consequence of the huge numbers crowding into the Church.[1] Harnack comes to the conclusion, based on the numerical data which have come down to us, that the church in Rome had 'probably doubled, perhaps quadrupled' in these fifty years.[2]

We advance one step farther when we observe that besides the Marcianus inscription we have three more on children's tombs from the third century which, like that of Marcianus, mention the child's age at the time of baptism, because these children, like Marcianus, had died quite soon after being baptized (J 78–80):

[1] A. von Harnack, *The Mission and Expansion of Christianity in the First Three Centuries*, ET[2], London, 1908, II, 324ff.
[2] *Op. cit.* II, 329.

Tyche (aged one year ten months fifteen days, died on the day of her baptism),[1] Irene (died when eleven months old, six days after her baptism)[2] and Apronianus (aged 21 months and three days, baptized *in extremis*).[3] All three inscriptions come from Rome, like that of Marcianus. Nothing can be gleaned from the Tyche inscription as to whether the parents were full Christians or catechumens. The situation is different in the case of little Irene, who was baptized on 7 April (unfortunately the year is not stated); here the date (Easter time) might indicate that the child had been baptized together with her parents on the occasion of the solemn Easter baptism at which the catechumen families were received into the Church (see above, pp. 28f.); but, since the baby died only six days after her baptism, it might equally have been a matter of an emergency baptism. On the other hand, it is not only 'admittedly possible' (A 77), but as good as certain that in the case of the third of these inscriptions, that of Apronianus, the father was a pagan. The inscription reads:

> *d(is) m(anibus) s(acrum)*
> *Florentius filio suo Aproniano*
> *fecit titulum benemerenti qui uixit*
> *annum et menses nouem dies quinque*
> *qui cum soldu amatus fuisset a maiore*
> *sua et uidit hunc morti constitutum*
> *esse petiuit de aeclesia ut fidelis[4] de*
> *seculo recessisset[5]*

> Dedicated to the divine *manes* (of the departed).
> Florentius made this inscription
> for his worthy son Apronianus who lived
> one year and nine months five days.
> As he was truly loved by his grandmother
> and she saw that his death was imminent,
> she asked the church that he might
> depart from the world as a believer.[6]

---

[1] Diehl, *Inscriptiones Latinae Christianae Veteres* I, No. 1531; F. J. Dölger, *ΙΧΘΥΣ* II, Münster, 1922, 521; J 79; A 77. Rome, catacomb of Priscilla.

[2] Diehl, *op. cit.* I, No. 1532; Dölger, *loc. cit.*; J 79; A 77f.

[3] Diehl, *op. cit.* I, No. 1343; Dölger, *op. cit.* II, 524; J 41f. Rome, catacomb of Priscilla.

[4] *Fidelis* means (from the time of Tertullian) the baptized Christian, as distinguished from *Christianus* (the catechumen).

[5] Cf. n. 3.   [6] J 42 (tr. by D. Cairns).

The strong emphasis on the circumstance that it was the grand-mother who insisted on the baptism of her darling as he lay dying leads us to the conclusion that Florentius, the child's father, who ordered the inscription, was not a Christian. A more definite pointer is supplied by the fact not noticed up till now that the expression 'she asked the church' (*petiuit de aeclesia*) makes use of a technical term employed for non-Christians applying for baptism.[1] This means that of the three inscriptions mentioned which, like that of Marcianus, give the child's age at the time of the baptism, the first one tells us nothing definite about the parents, the date in the second is a possible indication that it concerned a child of a catechumen, the third inscription refers almost certainly to the child of a pagan father. Thus in none of the three cases can it be proved that the parents were baptized Christians.

That they were so is, in fact, extremely improbable from the outset; this holds for the Marcianus inscription, too. For although we have numerous examples from the third century of the children of Christians being baptized as infants, yet on the other hand there is in the whole of the literature and the collections of inscriptions for the entire century not a single example of Christian parents delaying the baptism of their children. The Marcianus inscription would thus stand quite alone if it were conjectured with Aland (A 78) that the boy's parents were baptized Christians.[2]

[1] On the other hand, this cannot be deduced with equal certainty from the *d(is) m(anibus) s(acrum)*, as Aland rightly replies (A 77, n. 5), because this pagan formula does appear on Christian inscriptions of the third century, though very rarely.

[2] A word may be added as a note concerning the inscription in *Corpus Inscriptionum Graecarum* IV, Berlin, 1877, 551, No. 9715; J 56. It reads:

$$\text{'Aλκινόων δύο σῆμα 'Aλεξάνδρου τε συνέμων}$$
$$\text{τρεῖς ⟨δὴ⟩ δωδεχέτεις πιστοὺς γενετῇ προέπενψα}$$
$$\text{ιχθυς}$$
$$\text{γ}$$

On p. 76, n. 2, Aland comments on this: 'πιστοὺς γενετῇ προέπενψα' probably means, "I (the father or relative) have sent on (the three twelve-year-old) believers to the father (or relative)".' This translation, which, by the way, would require the accentuation γενέτη (not γενετῇ, as Aland writes), does not seem to me to be possible. Firstly Aland's rendering presupposes that the father spoke of himself in one breath first in the third person (γενέτη) and then in first (προέπενψα) which is quite improbable. Next the three boys of the same age are not brothers, but 'relations' (συνέμων); therefore they have different fathers. Aland tries to take this into account by translating γενέτη as 'father (or relative)'; but γενέτη cannot mean 'relative'. Above all προπέμπειν here means 'to accompany on the last journey'; in this case γενετη cannot belong to προπέμπειν. So the only alternative is to connect γενετη with πιστούς; thus the choice lies between πιστοὺς γενέτη ('loyal to the father') and πιστοὺς γενετῇ ('believers by birth'). The second possibility, which Wolf-Hartmut Friedrich also prefers, is supported, as A. Kirchhoff had

We have now exhausted our material. Thus we have failed in our search for trustworthy support for the hypothesis that in the first three centuries an age-limit was observed for the baptism of children.

4. INDICATIONS THAT THERE WAS NO AGE-LIMIT IN THE FIRST TWO CENTURIES

The conclusions of this chapter so far are to the effect that no support could be found anywhere for an age-limit observed for baptism in the first two Christian centuries. But we do not have to rely on this negative statement alone. On the contrary there are quite a number of indications that during this period children were baptized without an age-limit. I speak of indications, because baptism is not mentioned explicitly; besides, the passages vary in importance. Yet taken together they result in a fairly close network both chronologically and by their regional distribution. In my book, *Infant Baptism in the First Four Centuries*, I had presented them arranged geographically, and I do not intend to repeat what I said there. So I confine myself to producing additional observations, to commenting on Aland's objections and especially to examining the evidence from the point of view of the hypothesis that there was an age-limit for baptism.[1]

(a) *Exhortations to parents*

I must begin by drawing attention to a fact which has not been brought out up till now. It is very remarkable that in the exhortations

---

seen in 1877 (*Corpus Inscriptionum Graecarum* IV, *ibid.*), by the analogous phrase πιστὸς ἐκ πιστῶν ('a believer [born] from believers') of the Zosimus inscription (F. J. Dölger, *IXΘΥΣ* I², Münster, 1928, 201; J 56), which declares the two-year-old Zosimus to be a baptized child of Christian parents. So I translate the inscription thus:

'Burial mound of the two Alcinous and of Alexander, relatives.
Three twelve-year-old boys, believers from their birth, I accompanied on their last journey.'

Thus it remains an open question who is speaking. It is only stated that the three boys were baptized Christians (πιστοί, see p. 52, n. 4) and that they had Christian parents.

[1] As I shall not discuss Mark 10.13–16 and parallels in what follows, I will state in this note that Aland has completely misunderstood me in his chapter 9, 'The Blessing of the Children' (95–99), and has imputed to me the strangest opinions, as, for instance, that John 3.5 depends directly on Mark 10.15 (A 95f., 98), that Justin is dependent on Mark 10 (A 96), etc. Aland is confusing associations in the history of the tradition with literary dependence. That Matt. 18.3 and the parallel passages Mark 10.15, Luke 18.17 on the one hand and John 3.5 on the other are associated in the history of tradition is incontestable and even Aland cannot deny it (A 97f.).

to parents in the primitive Church[1] they are never urged to prepare their children for baptism by giving them instruction nor to be concerned about their baptismal teaching. If the children of Christian marriages had really not been baptized until they had received instruction (A 106f.) and 'when they had attained knowledge' (A 107), some such admonition would be expected at least in some passage or other. But none can be found anywhere.[2]

(b) Justin, Apology I, 15.6

We begin the scrutiny of the material with a very important statement by Justin which is worth examining more closely. In his *First Apology* Justin mentions 'many men and women sixty and seventy years old οἳ ἐκ παίδων ἐμαθητεύθησαν τῷ Χριστῷ' and who preserved their sexual purity during a long life (15.6). Since Justin writes in 150/55, these men and women were born between AD 80 and 95. We must begin by asking what is the meaning of ἐκ παίδων ἐμαθητεύθησαν τῷ Χριστῷ. Aland maintains that 'taken as it stands' it 'cannot possibly mean, "they had been baptized as infants"' (A 73), and he thereby gives the impression that this is how I translate it. I can only state that this is not so, as Aland must admit in the next sentence; in particular, the word 'infant' does not occur at all in the whole of my paragraph (J 72). Aland for his part asserts that ἐκ παίδων ἐμαθητεύθησαν τῷ Χριστῷ 'taken as it stands' means 'they had been instructed in Christian faith from childhood' (A 73). The wording makes this impossible. For the deponent passive μαθητεύε-σθαι does not mean 'to be instructed' but 'to become a disciple' and τῷ Χριστῷ does not mean 'in Christian faith'. On the contrary the literal translation is: 'who became disciples of Christ from their childhood onwards'. We must notice here that the juxtaposition of a phrase expressing duration 'from childhood' (ἐκ παίδων) with an ingressive one 'they became disciples' (ἐμαθητεύθησαν) represents a popular breviloquence, for which there are analogies in the New Testament, e.g. in Matt. 9.22b: ἐσώθη ἡ γυνὴ ἀπὸ τῆς ὥρας ἐκείνης (literally: 'she was healed from that moment', meaning 'instantly'); similarly 15.28b: ἰάθη ἡ θυγάτηρ αὐτῆς ἀπὸ τῆς ὥρας ἐκείνης ('her daughter was healed from that moment'); 17.18b: ἐθεραπεύθη ὁ παῖς

---

[1] E.g. Eph. 6.4; Col. 3.21; I Tim. 3.4, 12; *Did.* 4.9 par. *Barn.* 19.5; I *Clem.* 21.8; Polycarp, *Phil.* 4.2; cf. also Hermas, *Vis.* I, 3.1; II, 3.1.

[2] Cf. the collection of the material in W. Jentsch, *Urchristliches Erziehungsdenken* (Beiträge zur Förderung christlicher Theologie 45.3), Gütersloh, 1951.

ἀπὸ τῆς ὥρας ἐκείνης ('his son was healed from that hour'); John
11.53: ἀπ᾽ ἐκείνης οὖν τῆς ἡμέρας ἐβουλεύσαντο ἵνα ἀποκτείνωσιν αὐτόν
('from that day they decided to kill him', meaning: 'on that day'). In
all these cases the emphasis falls on the ingressive verbs; the phrase
expressing duration indicates that the effect was lasting.[1] Accordingly, the phrase which is occupying us, οἳ ἐκ παίδων ἐμαθητεύθησαν
τῷ Χριστῷ, means 'who became disciples of Christ as children (and
remained so ever since)'. This is not brought forward as a contentious
philological point, but it is a statement which has its significance and
its consequences. As we have seen again and again, Aland bases his
theory of an age-limit in the main on the assertion that all children
in the first two centuries were baptized only after having received
instruction, which excludes infant baptism. His chief evidence was
Aristides, *Apol.* 15.6, where however, as we had to demonstrate on
p. 45, the 'instruction' owes its existence to an erroneous translation;
there is no mention of it in either the Greek or the Syriac text. The
position is exactly the same in this passage. Aland deduces from his
rendering 'they had been instructed in Christian faith from childhood' that infants are excluded ('the answer "as infants" is excluded')
(A 73), simply because they cannot yet be instructed. But in this
passage, too, Justin, *Apol.* I, 15.6, there is again nothing about
'instruction' in the text. The second question to be asked is: what
does Justin actually mean when he says: ἐκ παίδων ἐμαθητεύθησαν τῷ
Χριστῷ? *Dial.* 39.2 gives more help here. In that passage Justin says
that God delays judgement 'because he recognizes that even now,
every day, people become disciples in Christ's name and leave the
path of error, people who receive gifts, each according to his worth,
(when they are) enlightened through the name of this Christ'
(γινώσκων ἔτι καθ᾽ ἡμέραν τινὰς μαθητευομένους εἰς τὸ ὄνομα τοῦ Χριστοῦ
αὐτοῦ καὶ ἀπολείποντας τὴν ὁδὸν τῆς πλάνης, οἳ καὶ λαμβάνουσι δόματα
ἕκαστος ὡς ἄξιοί εἰσι, φωτιζόμενοι διὰ τοῦ ὀνόματος τοῦ Χριστοῦ τούτου).
On this Aland, presumably misled by his abbreviated citation (he
replaces the middle part from καὶ ἀπολείποντας to εἰσί by dots),
says: 'the second part only of the sequence of thought relates
to baptism, the first does not' (A 73). Thus he applies μαθητευομένους
('become disciples') to baptismal instruction, φωτιζόμενοι ('enlightened') to baptism. However, as we have seen, μαθητεύεσθαι
does not mean 'to instruct'; besides the 'gifts' (δόματα) already

[1] J. Jeremias, ''Εν ἐκείνῃ τῇ ὥρᾳ, (ἐν) αὐτῇ τῇ ὥρᾳ', ZNW 42, 1949, 216, No. 5.

refer to the imparting of the Spirit at baptism, as the sequel shows. Above all, Aland has overlooked what Conybeare demonstrated more than sixty years ago, namely that the phrase μαθη-τευομένους εἰς τὸ ὄνομα τοῦ Χριστοῦ αὐτοῦ is an allusion to Matt. 28.19, or more precisely to the short form of this passage which Eusebius gives in all his pre-Nicene writings: 'Go, make all peoples disciples in my name' (πορευθέντες μαθητεύσατε πάντα τὰ ἔθνη ἐν τῷ ὀνόματί μου, i.e., without the command to baptize and the trinitarian formula).[1] The reference to Matt. 28.19 shows that already the first of the four successive phrases in *Dial.* 39.2 ('become disciples', μαθητευομένους) is concerned with baptism and this is corroborated by 'in the name' (εἰς τὸ ὄνομα) drawn from the baptismal terminology. Thus μαθητεύεσθαι in *Dial.* 39.2 denotes becoming a disciple with obvious reference to baptism. Accordingly in the passage under discussion, *Apol.* I, 15.6, ἐκ παίδων ἐμαθητεύθησαν τῷ Χριστῷ means not, as Aland wishes, 'they had been instructed in Christian faith from childhood' (A 73), still less, they grew up 'as members of a Christian family' (A 73)—the ingressive aorist, too, conflicts with both interpretations—but: 'they became disciples of Christ as children (through baptism)'. Now at last the third question can be asked: what in actual fact does ἐκ παίδων mean? Aland, who pleads for 'children of maturer years' (A 74), has completely neglected the context. In *Apol.* I, 15.1–8, Justin is concerned with sexual discipline (περὶ σωφροσύνης). In 15.6 and 7f. he adduces, as examples from life, two different groups in the Church which he contrasts with each other: the one consists of those who 'became disciples of Christ as children' (ἐκ παίδων ἐμαθητεύθησαν τῷ Χριστῷ) and 'remained uncorrupted' up to their old age; the others are 'the countless multitude of those who broke away from licentiousness and came to learn this [sexual discipline]' (τὸ ἀναρίθμητον πλῆθος τῶν ἐξ ἀκολασίας μεταβαλόντων καὶ ταῦτα μαθόντων). In other words Justin contrasts those born as Christians with those who became Christians. In the case of the former the value of the evidence for the Christians' superior morality lies in their life-long σωφροσύνη; in the case of the latter it depends on the complete change in their manner of life. Ἐκ παίδων, to which the dictionary gives considerable latitude, can apply in our passage, where it is being contrasted with those converted as adults,

---

[1] F. C. Conybeare, 'The Eusebian Form of the Text Matth. 28.19', *ZNW* 2, 1901, 275–88, here pp. 282f.

only to early childhood. Therefore the sentence in 15.6a runs: 'and many men and women sixty and seventy years old who had become disciples of Jesus in early childhood remained uncorrupted'. Since the use of 'become a disciple' ($\mu\alpha\theta\eta\tau\epsilon\acute{\upsilon}\epsilon\sigma\theta\alpha\iota$) in *Dial.* 39.2 definitely refers to baptism, our passage contains an allusion to baptism in early childhood. The date makes the evidence significant for it takes us into the last decades of the first century; admittedly it is only an indirect piece of evidence, because baptism is not mentioned *expressis verbis*.

(c) Other matters

Aland (A 72f.) passes very quickly over *Mart. Polyc.* 9.3, where it is said that Polycarp of Smyrna, when challenged to deny Christ, confessed in face of martyrdom (probably in 167/8): 'Eighty-six years I have served him, and he never did me any wrong. How can I blaspheme my King who saved me?' ($\dot{o}\gamma\delta o\acute{\eta}\kappa o\nu\tau\alpha$ $\kappa\alpha\grave{\iota}$ $\dot{\epsilon}\xi$ $\ddot{\epsilon}\tau\eta$ $\delta o\upsilon\lambda\epsilon\acute{\upsilon}\omega$ $\alpha\dot{\upsilon}\tau\hat{\wp},$ $\kappa\alpha\grave{\iota}$ $o\dot{\upsilon}\delta\acute{\epsilon}\nu$ $\mu\epsilon$ $\dot{\eta}\delta\acute{\iota}\kappa\eta\sigma\epsilon\nu\cdot$ $\kappa\alpha\grave{\iota}$ $\pi\hat{\omega}\varsigma$ $\delta\acute{\upsilon}\nu\alpha\mu\alpha\iota$ $\beta\lambda\alpha\sigma\phi\eta\mu\hat{\eta}\sigma\alpha\iota$ $\tau\grave{o}\nu$ $\beta\alpha\sigma\iota\lambda\acute{\epsilon}\alpha$ $\mu o\upsilon$ $\tau\grave{o}\nu$ $\sigma\acute{\omega}\sigma\alpha\nu\tau\acute{\alpha}$ $\mu\epsilon;$).[1] This confession does not indeed mention baptism. Yet it permits an inference to be made. For the other dates of Polycarp's life known to us make it extremely likely that eighty-six, the number of years, indicates his age.[2] Thus Polycarp reckons his 'service of Christ' from his birth. This shows at any rate that his parents were already Christians, or at least were converted quite soon after his birth. If his parents were pagans at his birth, he would have been baptized with the 'house' at their conversion. But even if his parents were Christians, the words 'service of Christ' for eighty-six years supports a baptism soon after his birth rather than one as a child 'of maturer years' (A 74), which according to Aland must have been the general custom, but for which there is no evidence at all.

The reference to the Christian *'teneri'* of Pliny's letter (about 112)[3] 'yields no information and at most relates to children of several years old' according to Aland (p. 72, n. 5). But why does it 'yield no information'? If Pliny is considering whether these 'tender' children are to be prosecuted for belonging to the Christian Church, it can be assumed that they had become full members of it by their baptism,

---

[1] F. X. Funk and K. Bihlmeyer, *Die Apostolischen Väter* (Sammlung ausgewählter kirchen- und dogmengeschichtlicher Quellenschriften II, 1.1)², Tübingen, 1956, 125.
[2] Cf. J 62f.
[3] *Ep.* X, 96.2 (M. Schuster, *C. Plini Caecili Secundi Epistularum libri novem, Epistularum ad Traianum liber, Panegyricus*², Leipzig, 1952, 355, ll. 11–13).

which does not support an age-limit at puberty or at a 'more mature' age. Is this 'no information'?

What was said about Polycarp applies to Polycrates of Ephesus, who in 190/91 writes to Rome concerning the dispute over Easter: 'I have now (lived), brethren, sixty-five years in the Lord, and have conversed with brethren from all over the world and have perused all the Scripture' (ἐγὼ οὖν, ἀδελφοί, ἑξήκοντα πέντε ἔτη ἔχων ἐν κυρίῳ καὶ συμβεβληκὼς τοῖς ἀπὸ τῆς οἰκουμένης ἀδελφοῖς καὶ πᾶσαν ἁγίαν γραφὴν διεληλυθώς).[1] Polycrates, too, does not mention baptism explicitly, but it seems to me out of the question that by sixty-five years he 'intends to indicate nothing more than his age (what a Christian possesses, he has "ἐν κυρίῳ")' (A 72f.). Everything to which Polycrates refers, that he is the eighth bishop in his family (stated just before),[2] his ecumenical connexions, his thorough study of the Scriptures, is surely intended to emphasize his spiritual authority; he will hardly wish to support this by boasting about his age, especially as he himself adds that he refers to his age because of his concern for his long and unimpeachable Christian standing.[3] This passage taking us back into the year 125/6 as the year of Polycrates' birth, also favours the conjecture that baptism took place soon after birth, rather than that there was an age-limit for baptism.

To the period before AD 150 belongs the alteration which the archetype of Codex Bezae (D)[4] made in the text of Acts 2.39: '(38) Be baptized every one of you . . . (39) for the promise is to us [instead of 'to you'] and to our [instead of 'to your'] children' (βαπτισθήτω ἕκαστος ὑμῶν . . . ἡμεῖν [instead of ὑμῖν] γάρ ἐστιν ἡ ἐπαγγελία καὶ τοῖς τέκνοις ἡμῶν [instead of ὑμῶν] D d Aug.). The promise attached to baptism of receiving the Spirit is thus in Codex Bezae (D) made to refer to Christians and their children, and, as I wrote on p. 72, this is most readily explained by the fact that for the redactor 'the baptism of Christian children was a custom taken for granted'. The variant, so Aland asserts, 'provides Jeremias with a witness to infant baptism "before AD 150" in the West' (A 85). Actually I do not say a word about 'infant' baptism, but I adhere to

[1] Eusebius, *Hist. Eccl.* V, 24.7.
[2] V, 24.6.
[3] V, 24.8: 'I have not become grey-headed in vain, but I have always walked in Christ Jesus' (εἰκῇ πολιὰς οὐκ ἤνεγκα, ἀλλ' ἐν Χριστῷ Ἰησοῦ πάντοτε πεπολίτευμαι).
[4] It follows from the agreement of D with *d* that the change did not originate with the scribe of Codex Bezae, but was already in front of him, since it is well known that *d* is translated from an ancestor of D.

the text, which speaks of τέκνα, 'children' (not of 'infants'). Aland tries to discredit the variant 'to *our* children' (τοῖς τέκνοις ἡμῶν, 2.39) by representing it as thoughtlessness on the part of D; he says that the Codex replaces or removes 'you' (ὑμεῖς) elsewhere, too, in Peter's speech 'in various other passages . . . even in contexts where it is quite impossible (as 2.22)' because it 'endeavours to make the text relevant by directly relating it to the reader or hearer' (A 85). 'I do not believe that we can draw such conclusions,' I must reply to Aland in his own words (A 85). Apart from our passage, other changes or omissions of 'you' (ὑμεῖς) in Peter's speech occur in 2.17 and 22,[1] and in both passages the alteration has been carefully considered. In 2.17 'your' (ὑμῶν) has been twice replaced by 'their' (αὐτῶν) and twice omitted in order to remove the limitation on the gift of the Spirit, and this has long been recognized; thus according to D it does not apply to the Jews alone, but to all men (πάσας σάρκας D). And in 2.22 the change from 'you' (ὑμᾶς) to 'us' (ἡμᾶς) ('a man approved by God for us through mighty deeds and miracles and signs'[2]) is 'quite impossible' in the context only if the mistake is made of referring 'for us' (εἰς ἡμᾶς) to the 'reader or hearer' (A 85); but in fact εἰς ἡμᾶς refers to the disciples: 'D changes ὑμᾶς to ἡμᾶς because only the disciples and not the Jerusalemites have experienced these wonders', as E. Haenchen states correctly.[3] Thus there can be no question of thoughtlessness in the case of both alterations (2.17, 22). In 2.39, too, the alteration from 'to your children' (τοῖς τέκνοις ὑμῶν) to 'to our children' (τοῖς τέκνοις ἡμῶν) is well considered; it is intended (as in 2.17) to detach the promise in Joel from the Jews; it is given not to Israel and its children but to the Christians and their children. That Codex Bezae elsewhere, too, lays special stress on children belonging to the Church is shown by two additions: between ἐβαπτίσθη καί and ὁ οἶκος αὐτῆς (16.15) D d insert a πᾶς ('she was baptized and *all* her household') and—even more clearly—instead of 'together with the women' (σὺν γυναιξίν, 1.14) D d (only these!) read 'together with the women and children' (σὺν ταῖς γυναιξὶν καὶ τέκνοις). The article before γυναιξίν in D indicates that with the γυναῖκες D is thinking of the wives of the eleven

---

[1] 2.14 ἡμεῖν D (instead of ὑμῖν) is a copyist's error, as *vobis d* shows; 2.33 ἐξέχεεν ὑμῖν ὅ D d (instead of ἐξέχεεν τοῦτο ὁ ὑμεῖς) is only an improvement for reasons of style; 2.38 does not belong here, because D shares the variant (om. ὑμῶν 2°) with many other witnesses.

[2] ἄνδρα ἀπὸ τοῦ θεοῦ [δεδοκιμ]ασμένον εἰς ἡμᾶς δυνάμεσι καὶ τέρασι καὶ σημίοις D d.

[3] *Die Apostelgeschichte*[13], Göttingen, 1961, 143, n. 1.

apostles previously mentioned. Now quite recently W. Thiele has drawn attention to the fact that the chapter heading of 1.12–14 found in several manuscripts of the Vulgate, and which goes back to a very ancient Old Latin text, speaks 'of the meeting of the apostles and the prayer they had together with their [the apostles'] nursing wives' (*de congregatione apostolorum et oratione quam cum altricibus suis mulieribus celebrabant*).[1] This chapter heading confirms not only that the reading of D *d* was applied to the wives of the apostles; but it teaches more than this, namely that καὶ τέκνοις was taken to mean either the infants only or (and this is more likely) the children of the apostles including the infants. In the latter case it is the complete families of the apostles who are imagined in 1.14 as gathered for prayer with Jesus' mother and brothers. Similarly D intends our passage (2.39) to be applied to the Christian 'houses'; the promise of the Spirit attached to baptism is made to the Christian parents and their children.[2]

Aland devotes a long discussion (pp. 70–72) to the confessions of the martyrs (about 165 and later). The point is that repeatedly martyrs back up their refusal to deny their faith by pointing out that it has been theirs from their youth up.[3] I had collected the evidence on p. 64 of my book (so far as I know for the first time from the point of view of this subject). I have read Aland's discussion with the greatest astonishment. He writes that none of these phrases refer to the time of infancy and that is his constantly recurring conclusion. Therefore a reader of Aland's book must suppose that I find in these confessions as many proofs of infant baptism. In fact, I do not say a single word about infant baptism, but I record these confessions as indirect evidence for the baptism of children. The martyrs who used

---

[1] W. Thiele, 'Eine Bemerkung zu Act 1.14', *ZNW* 53, 1962, 110 f.

[2] Aland is turning things upside down when he writes that 'when we see how D here and in various other passages endeavours to make the text relevant . . . we shall not be inclined to regard the change of text in 2.39 as reflecting a practice of infant- or child-baptism in that time' (A 85). The opposite is correct; it is just when it is seen that D makes the text relevant elsewhere that the same must be assumed for 2.39!

[3] ἀπὸ νεότητος θεῷ δουλεύω, παρὰ γονέων παρείληφα Χριστιανὸς εἶναι, ἀπὸ τῶν γονέων . . ., *ab ineunte aetate* . . . etc. To the evidence of the third century contained in n. 3 on p. 64 of my book might be added: *Martyrdom of Irenaeus* (Bishop of Sirmium) 4.3: 'I have a God whom I have learnt to serve from my earliest youth up' (*Deum habeo, quem a prima aetate colere didici*, Knopf-Krüger, 104.1); cf. *Martyrdom of Sabas* 1.3: 'For since he was a little boy he had never been a follower of anyone else than of the religion (that reveres) our Saviour and Lord Jesus Christ' (οὐ γάρ τινος ἑτέρου γέγονεν ἐξέτι νηπίου ζηλωτὴς ἀλλ' ἢ τῆς εἰς τὸν σωτῆρα καὶ κύριον ἡμῶν Ἰησοῦν Χριστὸν εὐσεβείας, Knopf-Krüger, 119.16f.).

the phrases quoted above were baptized Christians; they are not said to be receiving the baptism of blood; some of them say that they have inherited their faith from their parents. Their confessions show that they were not first converted as adults, but were Christians already from their youth up. That is all the texts prove. Nevertheless I mention them because they receive a more precise significance from the other texts.

Finally we come to Irenaeus, who writes soon after 180: 'For he (the Lord) came to save all of them through himself; all of them, I say, who through him are born again in God, the infants, and the small children, and the boys, and the mature, and the older people' (*omnes enim venit* [*Dominus*] *per semetipsum salvare: omnes inquam, qui per eum renascuntur in Deum, infantes, et parvulos, et pueros, et iuvenes, et seniores*).[1] By 'to be born again' (*renasci*/ἀναγεννᾶσθαι) and 'rebirth' (*regeneratio*/ἀναγέννησις), following the regularly accepted usage,[2] Irenaeus is denoting the regeneration granted in baptism.[3] This is abundantly established by the fact that he defends the connexion of rebirth with baptism passionately against the Marcosians.[4] So Irenaeus says that Jesus saves and sanctifies men of every age from infants (*infantes*) to old men (*seniores*) so far as they are baptized. Aland cannot deny that the *renasci* occurs at baptism. But he raises the objection that the context is not speaking of baptism, but of the sanctification of the several ages of life (A 58f.). He says of the context: 'It does not seem apparent to me that Irenaeus has baptism in view here, and certainly there is no thought of infant baptism; he is concerned solely with the fact that Jesus sanctified all humanity in that he was made like all, lived through all ages of life and was an example to all. . . . Nothing more than this is presupposed; nothing more than this is stated; therefore nothing more than this should be sought from it' (A 59). This objection misses the point completely. That baptism is not the theme of the section makes no difference to the fact that the subordinate clause 'who through him are born again in God' (*qui per eum renascuntur in Deum*) refers to baptism. This clause states that the sanctification of all the ages of life by Jesus, described in detail by the context, applies only

---

[1] *Adv. haer.* II, 33.2 (Harvey I, 330) or 22.4 in MPG 7, 784. Aland (p. 58, n. 3) inadvertently writes II, 23.2.
[2] Evidence in J 73, n. 2.
[3] Evidence in J 73, n. 3; see also Fragment XXXIII (Harvey II, 497f.).
[4] *Adv. haer.* I, 14.1 (Harvey I, 180–3).

to those who are baptized. In Aland's argument the context has suddenly made him forget this clause altogether. Yet this is the only thing that matters for our subject! Its brevity in no way reduces its importance. On the contrary the fact that the baptism of everyone, from the *infantes* to the *seniores*, occurs only in a subordinate clause, just shows how much Irenaeus takes it for granted that all, including infants, were baptized. No, if it is desired to escape from the conclusion that Irenaeus presupposes infant baptism in our passage, then the context gives no help. But another path must be followed: the five ages of life which Irenaeus enumerates (infants, children, boys, men, old men) must be interpreted allegorically. It has, in fact, been argued that the old men (*seniores*) might mean only an '*âge spirituel*'; because otherwise no parallel with Christ could be drawn, since he never reached the age of the *seniores*.[1] But now we have arrived at the place at which the context becomes important. If we read further we see that Irenaeus devotes the next two sections[2] entirely to proving in various ways (especially with the aid of John 8.57) that Jesus had nearly attained the age of fifty and therefore had, in fact, reached the age of *seniores* and thereby sanctified it. But if this way out by explaining the ages of life allegorically is closed, then we are left with the conclusion that by the subordinate clause 'who through him are born again in God' (*qui per eum renascuntur in Deum*) Irenaeus presupposes infant baptism as the practice of the Church—at any rate for Gaul, presumably also for his home, Asia Minor.[3]

To sum up, there is not a shred of evidence for Aland's hypothesis that in the first two centuries children were baptized only when they had reached an age at which they could receive instruction. But there are certainly quite a number of indications which argue against an age limit being observed at baptism. They vary in importance, but taken together they present a conclusive picture.

[1] A. Benoit, *Le baptême chrétien au second siècle* (Etudes d'Histoire et de Philosophie religieuses 43), Paris, 1953, 216f.
[2] *Adv. haer.* II, 33.3f. (Harvey I, 330–2).
[3] We must remember, too, that Hippolytus, whose *Apostolic Tradition* with its rules about the administration of baptism to small children was discussed on pp. 28ff., was most probably a disciple of Irenaeus.

IV

Infant Baptism
an Innovation about AD 200?

ALAND OFFERS one final argument for his assertion that infant baptism was not practised until the last years of the second century, and that on the contrary an age-limit for baptism was observed until then. His thesis is that Tertullian and Origen agree in revealing that at about AD 200 the custom of infant baptism was just being introduced. How does the matter stand?

I. TERTULLIAN

It is well known that in *De baptismo* 18.4f. (about 203) Tertullian encourages the postponement of baptism for small children (*parvuli*) as well as for virgins and widows: 'Why is the age of innocence in such a hurry for the forgiveness of sins?' (*quid festinat innocens aetas ad remissionem peccatorum?*).[1] That is perfectly clear. The important question for the history of the baptism of children arises only at this point. The question is: what situation does Tertullian's protest presuppose? Aland replies: 'In Carthage a significant tendency to baptize infants or young children is evidently in motion' (A 61). Tertullian is endeavouring 'by every means in his power to stem the tide of development towards infant baptism' (A 62). 'We catch a glimpse of the very beginnings of infant baptism in Carthage and Africa. About AD 200 there was a movement in that area that desired the baptism even of infants' (A 69). 'Obviously' Tertullian's demand to baptize children only 'when they are able to know Christ',[2] (actually, that is to say, for Tertullian, according to Aland, 'at the time of puberty') corresponds 'to the practice of the Church hitherto'

---

[1] *De baptismo* 18.5 (J. G. Ph. Borleffs, *Q .S.Fl. Tertulliani De baptismo*, CC 1.8, 1954, 293).
[2] *Cum Christum nosse potuerint, loc. cit.* (Borleffs, 293).

(A 106). We ask: is all this really 'obvious'? Can it be said that what Tertullian protests against is only a question of 'tendencies', of a 'movement' which would like to introduce the baptism of infants? There are three objections to this. Firstly, however cautiously the *argumentum e silentio* must be used, here it is pertinent. Tertullian when opposing the necessity for infant baptism is evidently at a loss for a good case, as we see from his 'rather tortuous argumentation' (A 62) that the godparents are burdened with a responsibility which they cannot be expected to bear. Would he have let slip the chance of pointing out that he was defending against attempts to introduce innovations the Church's good old custom of baptizing children only at the age of puberty, if this completely effective argument had been at his disposal? Secondly Tertullian substantiates his objection to the baptism of 'small children' (*parvuli*), as we have said, with the argument that the godparents would run a risk, since 'both they themselves might be prevented by death from redeeming their promises and they might also be deceived by the appearance of bad natural tendencies (in their godchildren)'.[1] This mention of the institution of *sponsores* who at the baptism of the *parvuli* gave binding guarantees (*promissiones*) for the future conduct of their godchildren gives us information about a baptismal rite practised in North Africa at the baptism of the *parvuli*. This is clearly a matter not of hypothetical constructions, but of a practice observed by the Church. The same applies, thirdly, to Tertullian's assent to emergency baptism. This concession, too, does not have in view a proposed innovation, but it is the only part of the regular practice of the Church which Tertullian is willing to retain. Now this means that in AD 200 infant baptism was the generally accepted practice in North Africa. When, fifty years later (251 or 253), Bishop Fidus proposes not to baptize infants until the eighth day after birth except in cases of necessity,[2] it must not be deduced from this 'that at that time in the African Church there was no absolute unanimity concerning the details of infant baptism; and that would provide a yet further hint that it was not a custom handed down from the earliest Fathers' (A 69). On the contrary the unanimous decision of the sixty-seven bishops present at the Synod of Carthage, that

---

[1] *De baptismo* 18.4 (Borleffs, *loc. cit.*).
[2] Cyprian, *Ep.* 64.2 (G. Hartel, *S. Thasci Caecili Cypriani Opera omnia* II, CSEL 3.2, 1871, 718).

baptism should take place, as always, on the second or third day after birth, demonstrates that infant baptism at this age was the practice universally observed and that no one knew any other, not even Bishop Fidus himself! The discussion was indeed exclusively concerned with the day and did not arise because the details of the practice of infant baptism were still in a state of flux; it arose because from his study of the Scriptures Fidus had arrived at the opinion that the time of baptism should be brought into line with that of circumcision (administered on the eighth day).[1] Consequently we have nowhere the slightest support for the theory that infant baptism in North Africa at about AD 200 had been a newly introduced custom; still less that there had existed merely a 'tendency' (A 61), a 'movement' (A 69), a 'tide of development towards infant baptism' (A 62).

*　　*　　*

Whatever else might be said about Tertullian is of secondary importance compared with this. His statement in *De spectaculis* 4.1 that the baptismal confession is made 'with our mouth' (*ore nostro*) by no means 'effectively prevents its inclusion in infant baptism', as Aland declares (p. 64). We have, in fact, just seen that in North Africa in the case of infants the godparent (*sponsor*) acted as a proxy. Again, Tertullian says in *De corona* 3.3 that the candidates for baptism refrained from the daily bath for a week, 'something which surely does not have infants in view' (A 64). But we have already established (pp. 38ff. above) that descriptions of the baptismal ritual traditionally started with the baptism of adults, if only for the reason that the rite had to be simplified for infants. This can be learned from the tractate *Gerim* just as well as from Hippolytus' *Apostolic Tradition*. Lastly, as regards *De paenitentia* 6.3–24, I willingly admit that on p. 81, l. 8, of my book I ought to have said 'repentance' instead of 'joining the Church' (a similar correction should be made on p. 87, see above p. 42, n. 3); yet this amendment is of no importance for the argument as a whole.

A word must still be said about *De anima* (although the baptism of children is not itself discussed in this tractate), because in *De anima* the well-known phrase about the age of innocence

---

[1] J. C. Didier, 'Saint Augustin et le baptême des enfants', *Revue des Etudes Augustiniennes* 2, 1956, 109–29, here 109.

for which baptism need not be so urgent (*quid festinat innocens aetas ad remissionem peccatorum?*, *De baptismo* 18.5) is more thoroughly defined and worked out. Tertullian here speaks of 'the paradise of integrity' (*paradisus integritatis*) out of which man is driven at the age of puberty (38.1f.). But he is far removed from understanding the 'innocence of childhood' in a careless, superficial sense. This is shown in *De anima* 39–41. 'Where could a man be found', Tertullian argues, 'who is not approached by the evil spirit which from the moment of birth lies in wait for the souls, as though invited to do so by all those superstitious practices at the confinement?' (39.1). 'So practically no birth is pure, at any rate among the heathen' (*nulla ferme natiuitas munda est, utique ethnicorum*, 39.3; *utique* cannot be translated by 'i.e.' as in A 65, because the word does not have this meaning, but it must be rendered, as by me, by 'at any rate',[1] 'at all events', 'or at least certainly'). 'Hence' (*hinc*, because in the case of children born to Christian parents the heathen customs performed at birth are omitted) the apostle can say in I Cor. 7.14 that *sancti* are produced in mixed marriages. But this must be qualified: these children are, as it were (*quasi*), intended for *sanctitas*. *Alioquin meminerat dominicae definitionis: nisi quin nascetur ex aqua et spiritu, non inibit in regnum dei, id est, non erit sanctus* (39.4 ad fin.): 'For the rest, he (the subject is Paul) had in view the stipulation of the Lord: unless a man is born of water and the spirit, he cannot enter into the kingdom of God, that is to say, he cannot be holy.' *Alioquin* ('for the rest') still refers to I Cor. 7.14; this is confirmed by the repetition of the key word *sanctus* at the end of the sentence (*id est, non erit sanctus*). By the statement that Christian children were *sancti* (more precisely *designati* for *sanctitas*) the apostle wished 'by no means' to deny that baptism is necessary to attain complete purity—this is how Waszink[2] correctly paraphrases the *alioquin* sentence in 39.4. Accordingly the sentence refers to the children of Christians (or to children with one Christian parent), whereas Aland in my opinion on pp. 65f. disrupts the train of thought by relating it to pagan children. The following sentence (*De anima* 40.1): that therefore 'every soul' (*omnis anima*) is impure until it has been entered on to Christ's list (*quamdiu recenseatur*), follows on

---

[1] J. H. Waszink, *Quinti Septimi Florentis Tertulliani De Anima*, Amsterdam, 1947, 440. The rendering 'i.e.' of *utique* on p. 446, which Aland follows, is inaccurate.
[2] *Op. cit.*, 440, 446.

smoothly and applies without restriction to all, not only to the children of pagans, as Waszink has again correctly seen.[1] It is true that the children of Christians differ from the children of pagans in that they are not stained at birth by superstitious customs, but they, too, have a share in the 'evil in the soul' (*malum animae*) which 'because of the original fault' (*ex originis uitio*) precedes the particular sinful actions (41.1: *malum igitur animae . . . ex originis uitio antecedit, naturale quodammodo. Nam, ut diximus, naturae corruptio alia natura est*). They, too, belong to fallen mankind whose 'total substance' (*uniuersam substantiam*) the devil 'changed into a state of rebellion against the Creator' (*in peruersitatem demutauit aduersus institutorem, De spectaculis* 2.12); they, too, are involved in the consequences of Adam's fall, of that *transgressio* which 'branded the whole man with the judicial record of his transgression, and therefore has deservedly filled him with perdition' (*totum hominem elogio transgressionis inscripsit atque exinde merito perditionis impleuit, De resurr. mort.* 34.1); they, too, have to suffer from the fact that Adam 'made his whole race, drawing contamination from his seed, a stock or breed tainted with his own condemnation' (*totum genus de suo semine infectum suae etiam damnationis traducem fecit, De test. anim.* 3.2).[2] Now this evil in the soul, brought by the fall and preceding particular sinful actions (*malum animae . . . ex originis uitio, De anima* 41.1), which is certainly not total, because the *bonum animae* counteracts it (*loc. cit.*), is blotted out together with the sinful actions at baptism; Windisch[3] and Oepke[4] had therefore assumed that Tertullian recommended infant baptism in *De anima*. I no longer believe that they were right about this. But on the other hand I am inclined to think that Aland is falling into the opposite extreme when he sums up Tertullian's opinion about the children of Christians in the statement that (as contrasted with the children of pagans) they are pure until puberty (A 67). Tertullian himself does not put it in this way, and Aland frankly reveals by his 'that surely means' (A 67) that he is here working with inferences. But the matter is hardly so simple for Tertullian! Even Christian children

---

[1] *Op. cit.*, 448: 'The sentence [40.1] is closely related to the *last* sentence of ch. 39' (W.'s italics). Waszink explicitly rejects the proposal (made by Aland on p. 65) that 40.1 refers back to 39.1–3.

[2] Cf. N. P. Williams, *The Ideas of the Fall and of Original Sin*, London, 1927, 239f.

[3] H. Windisch, 'Zum Problem der Kindertaufe im Urchristentum', *ZNW* 28, 1929, 135f.

[4] A. Oepke, 'Urchristentum und Kindertaufe', *ZNW* 29, 1930, 88f.

after all share in the 'evil in the soul' (*malum animae*) and Tertullian's sentence, 'every soul is impure until it has been entered on Christ's list' (*omnis anima . . . tamdiu immunda, quamdiu recenseatur, De anima* 40.1) does not contain the qualification 'however, for the children of Christians this only applies from puberty onwards'. For otherwise why did Tertullian approve of the emergency baptism of the *parvuli* (*De baptismo* 18.4)?

To return to our starting-point, namely whether Tertullian is writing against trends towards the introduction of infant baptism or against an already established custom, let us in conclusion quote N. P. Williams. Like ourselves he is of the opinion that Tertullian's objections are directed against an existing usage. In addition he gives an illuminating explanation of Tertullian's opposition to the Church's custom of infant baptism. Tertullian is acquainted, as Williams points out, with the idea of Adam's 'original sin' with all its depraving consequences for each of his offspring; but he has not yet developed an explicit doctrine of the 'original guilt' of Adam's descendants. Had he already known the idea of a hereditary responsibility for Adam's fall, it would of necessity have led him to assent to the baptism of the *parvuli*. But as he had not yet arrived at this idea, he could concentrate his attention completely on 'the terrible danger of post-baptismal actual sin which haunts those who receive the rite without long and searching preparation, and mature purpose; hence he vehemently urges the postponement of baptism in the cases of children and of unmarried adults'.[1]

2. ORIGEN

Origen is adduced by Aland as a second authority who is said to show that infant baptism—and actually as late as between 231 and 250!—was felt to be an innovation. 'When the attitudes he adopted to infant baptism are closely examined, it is clear that they all stand on the defensive against the belief that infants do not need baptism, on the ground that, as infants have not actually committed any sins, they do not require forgiveness of sins' (A 47). So there must have been influential circles who 'held a different opinion as to the necessity of infant baptism and who correspondingly maintained a different practice, in that they abstained from baptizing infants' (A 47). But in that case this custom between 230 and 250 in Palestine

[1] N. P. Williams, *op. cit.*, 241.

cannot have been very old. There is no other explanation for the fact that 'the voices against infant baptism are still so strong that Origen has to enter into discussion with them time and again' (A 48f.). Let us hear what Origen himself has to say!

Origen mentions infant baptism as the custom of the Church three times; in his *Commentary on the Letter to the Romans* he adds that the custom reached back to the apostles.[1]

The first of these three texts occurs in the fourteenth *Homily on Luke*, which expounds Luke 2.21–24. Here Origen is occupied with the striking sentence in 2.22: 'and when the days for *their purification* according to the law of Moses were fulfilled' (καὶ ὅτε ἐπλήσθησαν αἱ ἡμέραι τοῦ καθαρισμοῦ αὐτῶν). As a conscientious exegete, he cannot pass over the plural αὐτῶν, which today is still difficult to expound, since it is not clear to whom it refers. He finds himself forced to admit, although with great hesitation (*temerarie forsitan videor dicere, sed scripturarum auctoritate commotus*), that not only Mary, but also the newborn child Jesus 'needed cleansing and was unclean or stained by some kind of defilement'. He does indeed hasten to add that a careful distinction must be drawn between 'defilement' (ῥύπος, *sordes*) and 'sin' (ἁμαρτία, *peccatum*). If Jesus (like every newborn child according to Job 14.4f.) was infected with 'defilement', this expresses his real humanity! On the other hand, he had no sin. On account of the 'filthy garments' (Zech. 3.3) the legal sacrifice of purification had to be offered for him. Origen continues: 'On this occasion I should like to say another word concerning a question often discussed amongst the brethren. Infants (παιδία) are baptized for the remission of sins. What sins? Whenever have they sinned? In fact, of course, never. And yet: "no one is free from defilement [even if he is only one day old]" (Job 14.4f.). But the defilement is only put away by the mystery of baptism. That is the reason why infants (παιδία) too are baptized.'[2] We must notice in these last sentences (1) that Origen is incidentally taking up a problem frequently discussed 'amongst the brethren'; (2) that this problem

---

[1] Possibly two other passages should be added. The first is *Homily on Joshua* IX, 4 (on Josh. 8.32; Baehrens, GCS 30 (VII), 350.2–8): *et tu fuisti infans* (actually or metaphorically?) *in baptismo*. The second occurs in the *Commentary on Matthew* XV, 36 (on Matt. 20.1–16; Klostermann, GCS 40 [X], 457a.7–9; 458a.9): the workers hired at daybreak are here taken to mean τοὺς μὲν ἐκ παίδων καὶ πρώτης ἡλικίας κληθέντας, who shortly afterwards are called οἱ ἐκ παίδων πιστοί (their baptism is not mentioned, but is taken for granted).

[2] *Hom. on Luke* XIV (on 2.22, Rauer², GCS 49 [35] [IX], 87.18–88.8).

is not *whether* the infants should be baptized, but rather what *meaning* their baptism has, and (3) that nothing is said about the 'brethren' abstaining from baptizing infants.

A second explicit reference to infant baptism occurs in the eighth *Homily on the Book of Leviticus*. In Lev. 12.2–8 it is stated that after the birth of a boy the mother remains unclean for seven days. When a total of forty days has expired she must bring a burnt-offering and a sin-offering, and 'the priest shall make atonement for her, and she shall be clean' (v. 8). Why does the mother become unclean through the act of birth, so that she must make a sin-offering? 'I do not dare', says Origen, 'to make a pronouncement about these things, but I have a feeling that these regulations contain certain dark mysteries, and that a hidden and secret cause is the motive for calling a woman who has conceived and borne a child unclean and for obliging her to purify herself through a sin-offering, as though she had been guilty of a sin.' But the child, too, is not 'pure from defilement' at its birth, as Job 14.4f. shows. The mysterious stain connected with birth can be recognized also by the fact that according to the Bible only tyrants like Pharaoh and Herod Antipas celebrated their birthday, whilst Jeremiah and Job cursed the day of their birth. In addition to Job 14.4f., Ps. 51.5 (Heb. 51.7) also testifies that 'every soul that is born in the flesh is defiled by the stain of "unrighteousness and sin"' . . . In addition, we may in this context consider the question why it is that, though the baptism of the Church is given for the remission of sins, the Church's custom is to give baptism even to infants. For if there were nothing in the infants which needed remission and pardon, the grace of baptism would appear superfluous' (*quaecumque anima in carne nascitur, >iniquitatis et peccati< sorde polluitur . . . Addi his etiam illud potest, ut requiratur, quid causae sit, cum baptisma ecclesiae pro remissione peccatorum detur, secundum ecclesiae observantiam etiam parvulis baptismum dari; cum utique, si nihil esset in parvulis, quod ad remissionem deberet et indulgentiam pertinere, gratia baptismi superflua videretur*).[1] Origen is again dealing with an enigmatic scriptural pronouncement: that every mother is unclean when giving birth and must bring a sin-offering (Lev. 12.2–8). He admits that for him, too, the ultimate background of this regulation is mysterious. Yet scripture testifies that every newborn child (*quaecumque anima in carne nascitur*) is 'defiled by the stain of unrighteousness

---

[1] *Homily on Leviticus* VIII, 3 (on 12.2, Baehrens, GCS 29 [VI], 398.7f., 10–18).

and sin' (*iniquitatis et peccati sorde polluitur*). Thus Origen advances now one step further than in the *Homilies on Luke*, where with the child Jesus in mind he attributed to the newborn baby only defilement, but not sin. A final additional argument for the sinfulness of newborn children, thus Origen concludes his train of thought, is provided by the practice of infant baptism. Since baptism is administered for the remission of sins, it might be asked—Origen does not say that the question had actually been raised, but assumes the possibility of it—for what reason the *parvuli* also were baptized; its administration to infants might seem superfluous if newborn children did not already need forgiveness. This short passage about infant baptism must be considered in its context in order to form a correct estimate of it. It has no importance for its own sake, but is added quite incidentally (*addi his etiam illud potest*) as an appendix to a train of reasoning complete in itself. There can be no question of an attack on influential circles who dispensed with infant baptism. On the contrary Origen presupposes that the practice of infant baptism is so natural and undisputed that it can provide extra support to underpin his assertion based on Scripture that newborn children are tainted with sin.

Lastly, in the *Commentary on the Letter to the Romans*, when expounding the phrase 'the body of sin' (τὸ σῶμα τῆς ἁμαρτίας, Rom. 6.6), Origen once again comments on the regulation that a pigeon must be brought as a sin-offering for each newborn child (Lev. 12.6–8). 'For what sin?' 'Could a *parvulus* who has only just been born commit a sin? And yet he has sin for which it is commanded to offer a sacrifice', as Job 14.4f. and Ps. 51.5(= 51.7) show. 'For this reason the Church received from the apostles the tradition to administer baptism to the *parvuli* also. For the men to whom the secrets of the divine mysteries had been entrusted knew that in everyone (*in omnibus*) there were genuine sinful defilements, which had to be washed away with water and spirit.' On account of these defilements the body itself is called a 'body of sin', and this is not because of offences which the soul might perhaps have committed in another body during its transmigration.[1] We notice that in the *Commentary on the Letter to the Romans*, too, infant baptism is mentioned quite casually. It is again brought in as a supplementary confirmation of the sinfulness deduced from the witness of Scripture.

[1] *Commentary on the Letter to the Romans* V, 9 (on 6.5–7, MPG 14, 1047).

No polemic becomes evident. Origen presupposes that the custom of infant baptism is a matter of course; it is only on this assumption that he can expect his argument to carry conviction.

We have let the sources speak for themselves at some length in order to give a direct impression of the way in which Origen argues from infant baptism without any hesitation and expecting no disagreement. He certainly enables us to see, most clearly in the *Homilies on Luke*, that 'amongst the brethren' the question of its meaning was discussed. But that is explained by the change in the understanding of baptism. It had gradually lost its original eschatological significance; it had been restricted to the mediation of the remission of sins. If we bear in mind that throughout the whole of the second century and much later (evidence in A 105ff.) the belief in the innocence of newborn children prevailed (*innocens aetas* was the phrase in Tertullian, for instance), it is not surprising that the understanding of baptism as restricted to the forgiveness of sins necessarily brought with it the question: 'What then is the significance of baptizing infants?' But not the slightest support can be found for the idea that infant baptism itself appears to be an innovation (A 48f.) or that there were circles which dispensed with it (A 47). On the contrary, these hypotheses are excluded by the very natural way in which Origen uses infant baptism as an argument. He assumes it to be generally recognized that it is 'a tradition handed down from the apostles' (*traditio ab apostolis*), and in so doing he is probably thinking of John 3.5.

But Aland goes still further. According to his view, Origen enables us to see in the introduction of infant baptism a consequence of the idea that even newborn babes are sinful. This, however, is to stand the argument on its head. For in actual fact Origen argues the other way round: from infant baptism he infers that the newborn infants must be tainted, must, in fact, be sinful. I will let N. P. Williams speak once more: 'It is not the case that men said "Infants are infected from the womb with a hereditary taint; they must therefore be baptised as soon after birth as possible"; what they did say (after the custom . . . had become thoroughly established) was: "The Church actually does baptise infants as soon as possible after birth, and we cannot suppose that the Church does anything without good reason; therefore, infants must be infected from the womb with a hereditary taint." *Legem credendi statuit lex orandi :* there is no clearer instance of the control exercised by liturgical or devotional practice over the growth of dogma than that provided by the study of the relations between the custom of Infant Baptism and the doctrine of Original Sin.'[1] It was infant baptism which came first. It was the *lex orandi* which led the way; from it was deduced the *lex credendi*, the doctrine of the sinfulness of newborn infants, not the other way round! It was not infant baptism which was the innovation, but the doctrine of original sin which was substantiated by it. This doctrine supplied the *ex post facto* justification for the existing custom of infant baptism.

What is the position with regard to Origen's own baptism? Was he himself baptized as a small child? Were his parents, in fact, Christians? 'Whether he had been a Christian from his *youth* is not so much as hinted at in the sources, so far as my knowledge goes' (A 48). According to Aland we know only that his father Leonides taught the young Origen Christianity and that the latter was seventeen years old when his father suffered martyrdom in AD 202. 'Only a romantic conception of the early Church could assert that the martyr death of his father presupposed a long standing as a Christian. . . . If it be so wished, Leonides may be regarded as a Christian from his youth—although even to go as far as that is to forsake the foundation of the sources.' 'Not a word stands in them [the sources] about his grandfather' (A 48). This might sound as though the inference from the martyrdom of the father Leonides that he had long been Christian originated with me. I need hardly say that I did not write anything so foolish. But what is the position with regard to Aland's assertion that 'the sources' are silent on the question whether Origen was a Christian from his youth, that it 'is to forsake the foundation of the sources' if Leonides is regarded as a Christian from his youth and that 'not a word' stands in them about Origen's grandfather? The threefold appeal to the sources does not alter the fact that Aland is mistaken here. The sources are by no means silent! They speak, and indeed in violent controversy. It is Porphyry who first informs us about the religious status of Origen at his birth and about that of his forefathers. He declares in the third book of his treatise *Against the Christians* that Origen was

---

[1] N. P. Williams, *Ideas of the Fall and Original Sin*, 223. J. C. Didier, too, stresses the fact that the practice of infant baptism preceded the doctrine of original sin: *Le baptême des enfants dans la tradition de l'Eglise* (Monumenta Christiana selecta 7), Tournai, Paris, Rome and New York, 1960, 8.

'a Greek raised among Greeks' ("Ελλην ἐν "Ελλησιν παιδευθείς).¹ He is contradicted incisively by Eusebius, who retorts that to assert that Origen was a pagan by birth and a convert to Christianity (ἐξ 'Ελλήνων μετατεθεῖσθαι) is a sheer lie (ψευσαμένῳ δὲ σαφῶς).² The truth is that 'he inherited the Christian teaching from his fore-fathers' (ἐκ προγόνων).³ Finally Rufinus must be included amongst the sources, though he was only a translator, because he shows how the phrase ἐκ προγόνων was understood; he renders it 'from his grandparents and forefathers' (ab avis atque atavis).⁴ This could already have been read in my book (p. 66). Are none of these sources? Does ἐκ προγόνων not include at the very least parents and grand-parents? Does not avus mean grandfather? Whether the truth lies with Eusebius or his opponent, Porphyry, the enemy of Christians, is a matter for debate.⁵ But the contention that the sources are silent simply does not agree with the facts.

To sum up: neither Tertullian nor Origen nor Cyprian give us the slightest support for the hypothesis that infant baptism was an innovation in their time or was felt to be such. On the contrary they are unanimous in showing that it was then the natural and traditional practice of the Church. We have already seen on pp. 28ff. and 62f., respectively, that this holds for Hippolytus and Irenaeus as well.

¹ Quoted by Eusebius, *Hist. eccl.* VI, 19.7.
² VI, 19.9.   ³ VI, 19.10.   ⁴ *Ibid.*
⁵ Recently M. Hornschuh, 'Das Leben des Origenes und die Entstehung der alexandrinische Schule', *Zeitschrift für Kirchengeschichte* 71, 1960, 1–25, 193–214, has pronounced definitely in favour of Porphyry, though with too much assurance. For Porphyry, too, where we can check his statements, does not prove to be reliable in every case. At least his assertion that Origen was not yet a Christian when he was a pupil of Ammonius Saccas (in Eusebius, *Hist. eccl.* VI, 19.6) is certainly wrong. Perhaps Porphyry even deduced that Origen was pagan by descent merely from his association as a pupil with Ammonius Saccas?

V

The Theology of Baptism

HERE WE come to the parting of the ways.

Whoever shares Aland's opinion (1) that the New Testament texts concerning household baptisms (so far as they admit any inferences at all) have in mind 'adults exclusively' (A 93, and on this see pp. 12ff. above), (2) that in the ensuing period 'prior to the close of the second century AD' an age limit was observed and children were not baptized until 'they had attained knowledge' (A 107, and on this see pp. 33ff. above), and (3) that infant baptism was an innovation which was still felt to be such in the later part of the first half of the third century (A 46ff.; on this see pp. 64ff.)—whoever shares this opinion must explain how this new custom happened to come into being 'about AD 200 or shortly before' (A 106). Aland undertakes this explanation in chapter 10 of his book, 'When and Why was Infant Baptism Introduced?' (A 100–11).

Aland speaks first of external factors which he says led to the emergence of infant baptism at 'about AD 200 or shortly before' (A 106). Until towards the end of the second century the Church had grown 'quite definitely' 'through the entry of new converts'. But these had been 'most commonly' adults (A 102). Of course there had been at all times births in Christian marriages. But not until after the great influx into the Church which took place after 180 had 'the absolute number of the children born in it also greatly increased'. Hence it was not until about 200 that 'their "belonging" to the Church, i.e. their baptism, becomes an ever greater problem' (A 103). In my opinion these considerations are wholly unconvincing. How can it be said that 'most commonly' adults were converted? Where did they leave their children? Surely they brought them with them? And so far as the children born within the Church are concerned, Aland cannot, as we have already seen on p. 47, appeal to Aristides, *Apol.*

15.6, for the strange assertion that at the beginning of the second century their number was 'not particularly large', that indeed children were 'not as the rule' assumed for Christian families (A 58). Moreover Aristides adds in 15.11 that the Christians 'thank God' at the birth of a child. There is not the least reason to suppose that the Church until the last years of the second century was essentially an adult church and that this situation was only altered after the influx which began in 180. Besides, why is it that the 'problem' of the baptism of children should have sprung up only with regard to the children born in the Church, and not also, and indeed particularly, with regard to the children of the converts? After all these had been born 'unclean' (ἀκάθαρτα in I Cor. 7.14c); they had been handed over at their birth, as Tertullian explains at length in *De anima* 39, by superstitious customs to the dominion of the powers of darkness. In their case the problem of baptism was bound to spring up urgently —and, of course, from the beginning! Therefore conjectures as to the proportion of children in the Church hardly serve to explain the alleged 'rise' of child or infant baptism at AD 200. On the contrary, we see from the stories about children in the Gospels, as well as from Acts 21.5, 21; I Cor. 7.14; Eph. 6.1, 4; Col. 3.20f.; I Tim. 2.15; 3.4, 12; 5.4, 10, 14; Titus 1.6, that children have from the very outset played a significant part for the Church, to say nothing of the accounts concerning household baptisms (which were dealt with in chapter I).

Now Aland himself, too, does not consider this attempt to explain the 'emergence of infant baptism' to be adequate (A 103). In his opinion it was an inner motive which was decisive. The primitive Church subscribed to the 'view of the purity of the new-born child'. Perhaps Jesus already held it (Mark 10.14f. and par.); certainly Paul did so with his view 'represented in I Cor. 7.14, that the children of mixed marriages (and correspondingly of Christian marriages) are ἅγια' (A 104). For the next period Aland adduces evidence for the view of 'the innocence of childhood' from the Apostolic Fathers and the Apologists (A 105f.). And then he draws a far-reaching conclusion: 'So long as and wherever this assumption held good, infant baptism was plainly not necessary, indeed it was superfluous' (A 106, similarly 104). 'For baptism is a bath of cleansing, in which a man is washed clean from his sins. If a child born of Christian parents is sinless [Aland does not say anything at this point about the children born before their parents' conversion!], it does not need this bath of cleansing' (A 104). For the last day 'will take the sinless infants and little children immediately to God' (A 106). We have already reported on pp. 33ff. what Aland considers the effect of this to have been on the practice which took shape during the first two centuries. It can be inferred from Tertullian, *De baptismo* 18.5 (between AD 200 and 206): 'So let them come when they are bigger, when they (can) learn, when they (can) be taught where to come; let them become Christians when they are able to know Christ' (*ueniant ergo dum adolescunt, dum discunt, dum quo ueniant docentur; fiant Christiani cum Christum nosse potuerint*).[1] 'Obviously that corresponds not only to what he believes to be right but to the practice of the Church hitherto' (A 106). Therefore this is how the Church proceeded: 'instruction was given and baptism administered to children when they had attained knowledge, at an age that required cleansing through the awakening of sin and destruction of original purity' (A 107)—if we follow Tertullian, then this is 'at the age of puberty' (A 111). Yet a complete change in the situation occurred when at the end of the second century the doctrine of original sin began to be developed. 'From the moment that the taint of original sin was believed to apply to the newborn child, its baptism became a necessity under the new presuppositions, for [here a second additional factor is introduced] it could no longer be assumed that the Last Day would come in the lifetime of these children. So far as we are able to judge from the sources, this fundamental change was completed about AD 200 or shortly before' (A 106).

However plausible this survey of the development may seem at the first glance, yet closer examination shows it to be untenable. It must be realized that the view which according to Aland was predominant in the first two centuries—'because children are innocent, they do not need baptism; they need it only when sinfulness awakens, that is to say, at a more advanced age'—is supposed to have gone back to the earliest times of the Church. The beginnings are what matter, *they* are decisive; that is when the points and signals are set which determine the course of the subsequent period. Hence we must frame our question thus: Does the view that the innocence of children was bound to make baptism appear 'plainly not necessary, indeed . . . superfluous' (A 106) pass the crucial test of the New Testament?

[1] Borleffs, CC 1, 293.

Let us begin with the 'innocence of childhood'. It is predicated in the second century of 'little children' (παιδία),[1] more precisely of 'infants' (νήπια),[2] of 'babes' (βρέφη),[3] of *infantes*[4] and of 'very small children'.[5] In other words, the authors named speak throughout not about the 'innocence of childhood' at all, but about the 'innocence of infants'.[6] If we wished to infer an age-limit for baptism from this 'innocence of infants', we should arrive at the age of one year, at the most two, but certainly not at the age of 'children of maturer years' (A 74), let alone puberty! Besides, it would still be necessary to ask whether the view that infants are innocent is already found in the New Testament. In the case of the second-century authors just cited, especially Hermas, who is particularly fond of the comparison with the innocent child, a part is played by a naive attitude common to the contemporary world 'which glorifies the innocence of childhood in a romantic fashion' (A 108). The New Testament does not do this anywhere. At all events it will not be possible to appeal to Jesus. For when in his two comparisons, 'the Kingdom of God is for such as these' (τῶν γὰρ τοιούτων ἐστὶν ἡ βασιλεία τοῦ θεοῦ, Mark 10.14 and par.) and 'whoever does not receive the Kingdom of God like a child' (ὃς ἂν μὴ δέξηται τὴν βασιλείαν τοῦ θεοῦ ὡς παιδίον, Mark 10.15 and par.), Jesus speaks of becoming a child again as the prerequisite for having a place in God's kingdom, it is quite improbable that moral integrity forms the *tertium comparationis*; possibly it is the smallness of the child, but still more probably the childlike simplicity, which can say 'Abba' to God. It would be more reasonable to appeal (with A 104, n. 4) to I Cor. 14.20 and I Peter 2.2 for the 'innocence of childhood'. 'Brethren, do not be children in your thinking, be babes in evil, but in thinking be mature': this is what Paul writes in I Cor. 14.20. The sentence in the middle 'be babes in evil' (τῇ κακίᾳ νηπιάζετε) is inserted as a parenthesis between the antithetical 'children in thinking/mature in thinking' (παιδία ταῖς φρεσίν/ταῖς φρεσὶν τέλειοι) and is altogether incidental, at this particular point and also in the context of the chapter which deals with glossolalia. Paul was quite

---

[1] *Barn.* 6.11.   [2] Hermas, *Mand.* II, 1; *Sim.* IX, 29.1.
[3] *Sim.* IX, 29.1, 3.   [4] *Sim.* IX, 31.3.
[5] Athenagoras, *De resurrectione mortuorum* 14 (ed. E. Schwartz, TU 4.2, 1891, 65.12): τοὺς κομιδῇ νέους παῖδας; cf. τοὺς κατὰ τὴν πρώτην ἡλικίαν τελευτήσαντας (65.13f.).
[6] Cf. the rabbinic expressions: blameless as 'a child one day old' (*Gerim* 2.6); 'as a child one year old who has not yet tasted the savour of sin' (*b. Yoma* 22b).

79

certainly not intending to make a theological pronouncement about the sinlessness of children, but he is putting before the Corinthians as an example in passing—according to the current usage[1]—the inexperience and unaffected simplicity with which the child faces the wickedness of men. And when in I Peter 2.2 the newly baptized are compared with 'newborn infants' (ἀρτιγέννητα βρέφη), the thought of the guiltlessness of a newborn infant could very well have played a part; in fact, however, the simile is used in quite a different sense: 'Crave like newborn babes for the genuine spiritual milk' (ὡς ἀρτιγέννητα βρέφη τὸ λογικὸν ἄδολον γάλα ἐπιποθήσατε)—the impetuous longing of the babe for its mother's breast is a simile for the vehemence with which the newly baptized are to desire the spiritual food (of the redemptive word). Finally Rom. 7.9 could also be brought in: 'I was alive without the law once' (ἐγὼ δὲ ἔζων χωρὶς νόμου ποτέ). But this passage points rather in the opposite direction; the sentences on either side of it speak with all seriousness of how sin lives in man from the beginning, even if it is dead at first, just as according to rabbinic ideas the bad impulse (different from the good one which begins to be active only when the age of thirteen years has been reached) dwells in man from birth, or even, according to Gen. 8.21, from conception.[2] On no account may Paul be set without further ado beside Pelagius, as he is by Aland on p. 104. He cites here the Pelagian doctrine 'that the newborn infants are in the state in which Adam was before the fall' (*quod infantes, qui nascuntur, in eo statu sint, in quo fuit Adam ante transgressionem*)[3] and comments on it that 'this estimate of the age of infancy can be demonstrated to go back to the beginnings of the Church'. 'To this context belongs the view of Paul, represented in I Cor. 7.14' (A 104). But there is nothing about this in I Cor. 7.14. For firstly Paul does not in the least assert of children in the mass, like Pelagius, that they are in a state of purity as in Paradise; on the contrary he says that the children of pagans are not pure; they are 'unclean' (ἀκάθαρτα). And secondly the 'holy' (ἅγια) which is affirmed of children of mixed marriages in I Cor. 7.14c does not denote moral integrity, as it was possessed by Adam before the fall; for after all it is placed beside the 'consecration' of the pagan partners in the mixed marriages (I Cor. 7.14ab) who are consecrated not because they are pure and innocent

[1] G. Bertram, νήπιος, νηπιάζειν, *TWNT* IV, 914, 918f. [2] Str.Bill. IV, 468f., 470f.
[3] Accusation of the Synod of Carthage of 411 (A 104, n. 2).

but because through their conjugal association with their Christian husband or wife they are in touch with the new creation in Christ. In *this* sense the children of mixed marriages are also consecrated because they descended from and live in the companionship of the Christian father or Christian mother. This consecration (ἡγίασται) or holiness (ἄγια) is therefore thought of as eschatological, not moral. It does not, as might be supposed, exclude baptism, at any rate in the case of the pagan conjugal partners, but is intended to lead to it: the Christian partner of the marriage has the desire and the obligation to 'save' the 'consecrated' pagan husband or wife, i.e., to bring him or her to believe and to be baptized (I Cor. 7.16).[1]

No! Truly there is nothing to be read in the New Testament about an 'optimistic view' (A 107) which knows about 'sinless infants and little children' whom the Last Day will take 'immediately to God' (A 106), and nothing at all about an innocence of childhood which would apply to pagan children as well and which they would, so to speak, bring with them at the conversion of their parents; nor is there anything about an innocence which would not be lost until 'more advanced' childhood, perhaps not even until fourteen years of age! Everything depends on the New Testament beginnings (this must be stated once more); it is they which determine the subsequent period.

But even if we assume that the view of the innocence of infancy as we find it in Christian writers of the second century could be traced back to the earliest days of the Church (although we could not discover any evidence for this), would the conclusion which Aland draws then be justified, namely that the baptism of innocent children 'was plainly not necessary, indeed it was superfluous' (A 106)?

Aland writes on p. 104: 'If a child born of Christian parents is sinless, it does not need this bath of cleansing (i.e. baptism).' But what is the position of children born to pagan parents before their conversion? They are born as τέκνα ἀκάθαρτα (I Cor. 7.14c). In consequence of the superstitious practices to which they were subjected at their birth they are nearly all defiled, says Tertullian, deflecting the Pauline thought from the sphere of eschatology into that of demonology.[2] Why is it that these defiled children 'do not

---

[1] Cf. *ad loc.* J. Jeremias, 'Die missionarische Aufgabe in der Mischehe (I Cor. 7.16)' in *Neutestamentliche Studien für Rudolf Bultmann* (BZNW 21), 1954 = [2]1957, 255-60.
[2] *De anima* 39 (see above, p. 67).

need this bath of cleansing' when their parents are converted? Where do we have the slightest support for the hypothesis that the pagan 'houses' were split up at baptism by excluding the 'sinless children' from the sacrament until they had reached an age limit? Questions would also arise with reference to the children born of Christian parents. How long did the innocence of newborn babes last? Where in the sources is it extended to a 'maturer age'?

But enough of this! In the last resort something else, a fundamental theological question, is at stake, namely the New Testament understanding of baptism. 'Baptism is a bath of cleansing, in which a man is washed clean from his sins' (A 104)—that is the crucial sentence in Aland's book, by which finally all stands and all falls. Aland himself has the feeling that something is not quite right here and so he adds in a footnote to it: 'Naturally the theological understanding of Christian baptism goes beyond this assertion, nevertheless in its basic significance baptism remains a bath of cleansing' (A 104, n. 1)—without making his case any better.

To put it at once perfectly clearly and unambiguously: it is the decisive weakness of Aland's book that it projects back into the apostolic period the shrivelled understanding of baptism which made its appearance in many places, though by no means everywhere, in the second century. Popular Hellenistic Christianity lost much of the understanding of the eschatological significance of baptism and saw in it to an increasing extent only the sacrament of the great remission of sins. A superstitious misconception of baptism, which regarded it merely as a charm by means of which forgiveness granted once for all could be obtained, became more and more common. The alarming extent to which this misunderstanding had spread is shown by the custom of postponing baptism which came into use in the fourth century. To be baptized if possible only on one's deathbed! To die if possible *in albis*! 'Let him be; he may do what he likes; after all he has not yet been baptized!' 'Disasters are threatening us from all sides, let us baptize our children as quickly as possible!'[1] What a falling away from the New Testament understanding of baptism!

Of course I have no intention of denying that from the very beginning to appropriate the forgiveness of sins was an essential part of the redemptive grace bestowed in baptism. Baptism is indeed

[1] Evidence on pp. 87ff. of my book.

'a bath of cleansing, in which a man is washed clean from his sins' (A 104). 'You were washed', writes Paul in I Cor. 6.11, and no statement about baptism recurs so frequently in New Testament writings as this one. Historically too baptism has its roots (from whatever source one might trace its origin in the history of religion) in the cultic bath of cleansing. But it is true already of proselyte baptism that cleansing is, so to speak, only the negative aspect of the effect of baptism; in its essential nature proselyte baptism is new birth, resurrection from the dead, being drawn into holiness ($q^e du\check{s}\check{s}a$).[1] The position is no different in the case of John's baptism, at any rate according to the Gospels (Josephus differs). John's baptism is a 'baptism of repentance for the remission of sins' ($\beta\acute{a}\pi\tau\iota\sigma\mu\alpha$ $\mu\epsilon\tau\alpha\nu o\acute{\iota}\alpha\varsigma$ $\epsilon\grave{\iota}\varsigma$ $\check{a}\phi\epsilon\sigma\iota\nu$ $\acute{a}\mu\alpha\rho\tau\iota\hat{\omega}\nu$, Mark 1.4; Luke 3.3). But yet it is not only this! Its essence is something else, namely deliverance from the menacing judgement of wrath (Matt. 3.7; Luke 3.7). It is a primary quality of John's baptism to be an eschatological sacrament.

It is even more true of the baptism 'upon Jesus' that it is an eschatological sacrament. The passage from I Corinthians quoted above does not say only: 'But you were washed'; it continues: 'but God[2] sanctified you, but God[2] justified you through[3] the Lord Jesus Christ and the Spirit of our God' (I Cor. 6.11). This statement about baptism has points of contact with the traditional liturgical language of baptism[4] and it reveals at once a fundamental characteristic of nearly all the statements about baptism in the New Testament, namely, their double-sidedness: 'Old things are passed away; behold, all things are become new' ($\tau\grave{a}$ $\acute{a}\rho\chi\alpha\hat{\iota}\alpha$ $\pi\alpha\rho\hat{\eta}\lambda\theta\epsilon\nu$, $\iota\delta o\grave{v}$ $\gamma\acute{\epsilon}\gamma o\nu\epsilon\nu$ $\kappa\alpha\iota\nu\acute{a}$, II Cor. 5.17). It is only necessary to call to mind the profusion of phrases and similes used in the New Testament as interpretations of the baptismal rite and the doctrine of baptism in order to recognize this 'double-sidedness', and at the same time to realize that the whole emphasis lies in each case without exception on the second halves. Baptism, to mention only what is most important, is not merely a bath of cleansing, but it is also a crossing of the waters into safety,[5] an action which saves from perdition[6] and

---

[1] Evidence in J 32–36.
[2] The passives paraphrase God's action.
[3] '$E\nu$ $\tau\hat{\omega}$ $\acute{o}\nu\acute{o}\mu\alpha\tau\iota$ = $b^e\check{s}em$ = through.
[4] This is the only place where Paul says $\grave{\epsilon}\nu$ $\tau\hat{\omega}$ $\acute{o}\nu\acute{o}\mu\alpha\tau\iota$ with reference to baptism, and where $\acute{a}\pi o\lambda o\acute{v}\epsilon\sigma\theta\alpha\iota$ occurs in his writings.
[5] I Cor. 10.1f.; I Peter 3.19–21.
[6] Acts 2.40; 16.30; Eph. 2.5, 8; I Peter 3.20f.

a change of lordship;[1] it gives a share in the benefits of Christ's atoning death (according to Rom. 6.3 this is pre-Pauline!);[2] it mediates the Spirit;[3] it is a new creation;[4] it is being born anew[5] and receiving the eschatological seal;[6] it is incorporation into the body of Christ,[7] union with the commonwealth of God's people[8] and admission to God's covenant through a 'Christian circumcision';[9] it is imparting the inheritance[10] and the life;[11] it is a divine legal act of justification[12] and of adoption;[13] it is sanctification,[14] enlightenment[15] and putting on the new garment, namely Christ.[16] In short, it bestows a new existence, because it includes in the dominion of Christ; it is actualized eschatology, receiving in anticipation, or rather antedonation, the complete fulfilment of salvation. And this baptism is supposed to tolerate an age-limit, is supposed to be 'not needed' (A 104) for infants and small children until they reach a mature age, to be 'plainly not necessary, indeed . . . superfluous' (A 106) for them! And this is supposed to have been done by people who from their past life regarded it as natural to be admitted into the covenant of God on the eighth day of life by the seal of circumcision and who looked upon baptism as the circumcision of Christ and the seal of God!

One last thing remains to be said. In the New Testament period baptismal grace, as salvation out of this world which is lying under the judgement of God, and incorporation into God's new world which is already coming into being, is experienced as a totality. Any consideration which isolates individual aspects, such as the forgiveness of sins or the bestowal of the Spirit, and inquires about the application of these to infants, overlooks the wholeness of the New Testament theology about baptism, as well as its basic eschatological character.[17] The very same wholeness of thinking also applies

---

[1] Col. 1.13. [2] Rom. 6.1-11; Eph. 2.5f.; Col. 2.12, 20; 3.1.
[3] Acts 1.5; 2.38; 9.17; 11.16; 19.5f.; I Cor. 12.13; II Cor. 1.22.
[4] II Cor. 5.17; Gal. 6.15.
[5] John 3.5; Titus 3.5; I Peter 1.3, 23; 2.2.
[6] II Cor. 1.22; Eph. 1.13; 4.30; cf. Ezek. 9.4, 6.   [7] I Cor. 12.13.
[8] Eph. 2.12f., 19.   [9] Col. 2.11.   [10] Gal. 3.29; Titus 3.7; I Peter 1.4.
[11] Col. 3.3f.   [12] I Cor. 6.11.   [13] Gal. 3.26; cf. Rom. 8.15; Gal. 4.6.
[14] I Cor. 6.11.   [15] Heb. 6.4; 10.32.   [16] Gal. 3.27; cf. Col. 2.11.
[17] A book which illustrates this point is G. R. Beasley-Murray's *Baptism in the New Testament*, London, 1962, which loses sight of the eschatological character of baptism by paying too much attention to its separate aspects. This extensive work, admittedly denominationally orientated, makes comprehensive use of the literature on the subject, but draws on the sources only at second hand and for this reason is not able, in the last resort, to further the discussion very much.

to the Christian community and their families. The whole people of God were baptized when they passed through the Red Sea (I Cor. 10.1f.), the whole family of Noah was saved in the ark, symbolizing baptism (I Peter 3.20f.); the promise of the Spirit is referred to the 'houses' ('to you and your children', Acts 2.39). They are seen as one unit in the sight of God. The faith of the father of the 'house' as representing his family, along with the faith of the mother, embraces the children as well, and the universal character of Christ's grace reveals itself in that it is the 'houses' which are summoned to believe and are baptized.

(excluding canonical OT passages from the lists pp. 19–25)

OLD TESTAMENT AND APOCRYPHA

INDEX OF SOURCES

INDEX OF MODERN AUTHORS